DOG PARKING IT!

A comprehensive Guide to fenced dog parks in California

by Gail S. Green, CPDT

ISBN 978-1-60264-408-3

Published 2009 by Virtualbookworm.com Publishing Inc.,
P.O. Box 9949, College Station, TX 77842.

Disclaimer: In the preparation of this book (*Dog Parking It!* – hereafter known as THE WORK), sincere effort has been made to record the most current, correct and clearly expressed information possible. All opinions expressed are those collected on the day of the visit, generally one visit, and are derived from the experiences of the author on that particular date. Even with this effort, inadvertent errors in information may occur. In particular but without limits the author, photographers, artists, publishers, printers, agents, heirs and associated involved in all aspects of THE WORK disclaim any responsibility for typographical mistakes, and the accuracy of the information that may be contained in THE WORK. The information and data included here, or in any publication associated with THE WORK, come from a variety of sources and are subject to change without notice. None of the persons, businesses or entities offer any warranties or representations whatsoever regarding the content, completeness, suitability, quality, sequence, accuracy, any and all services mentioned and/or suggested, or timeliness of such information and data.

There are possible references to services, veterinarians, groups representing some of the parks listed here. The references are not under the control of any of the aforementioned entities, and there is no inference of responsibility or liability for the actions of these organizations, institutions or companies. The user assumes all risks associated with the use of THE WORK, and mentioned parks or services, including veterinarian clinic and hospital care or advice. The creators and advisors of this book shall not, in any event, be liable for any direct, indirect, punitive, special, incidental or consequential damages, including, without limitation, lost revenues or profits, injury or illness to any animal, human or property arising out of or in any way connected with the use or misuse of the information or lack of information in THE WORK.

None of the associates involved in the creation and/or distribution of THE WORK and any services and entities mentioned in THE WORK endorse any of the mentioned services, or specific commercial products, processes, or service by trademark, trade name, manufacturer or otherwise.

The opinions expressed in THE WORK are solely the ideas, thoughts, feelings and understanding of the author and do not reflect positive or negative responsibility for the interpretation of parks or services as verbalized or written in THE WORK or any publication, broadcast, or other media entity in connection with THE WORK. The author and all services, businesses, and producers of THE WORK shall hold no liability or responsibility of slander of any park location, services or amenities or cautions as expressed in THE WORK and all related materials generated by or of THE WORK.

Book page and cover design: Gail S. Green
Cover and interior photographs of Twyla: Jack Van Voast
All Ragle Ranch Dog Park photographs: Lucy Aron

DOG PARKING IT!

A comprehensive guide to fenced dog parks in California

by Gail S. Green, CPDT
(Certified Professional Dog Trainer—KA)

For integration of each park location online with
GoogleEarth®, use this website, and click on
Dog Parking It! on GoogleEarth® :

www.berrygrovedogs.com

A portion of the proceeds from this book donated to
Valley Oak SPCA, Visalia, CA
www.vospca.org

Dedication

Yes, I have a GPS navigation device.

No, this is not dedicated to my GPS navigation device.

What I have found to be true is that mothers pushing strollers, couples walking their dogs, bicycle riders with spandex and helmets, and sweaty, drippy joggers all have been most helpful and courteous during this venture. I would often stop the car, roll down the window, and ask "Do you know where… ?"

Never has anyone refused to try to help. Except one guy that pointed to the ear buds in his head and waved me off.

And no one told me to get a map.

Thank you to all you sweaty people.
I am indebted to you, and to you I dedicate this book.

"Twyla" - photograph by Jack Van Voast, Mosswood Dog Park

Acknowledgments

Helen A. Green (also known as Ma): You are my best friend. Even when you tell me things I don't want to hear. Thanks for the incredible work you did, on me—and this book. I think Pa is looking down, grinning with his eyes and saying "Good on ya."

Michael T. Green and Family: My lil' bro and his pack. You spent many evenings helping me with this project, explaining to a computer idiot just how the "Earth" works. Thanks. Hugs.

The Whole Green Clan and Their Packs: Let's always be there to critique, compliment and make each other better. You are the very best. And I love each and every one of you.

Valerie Schillaci-Levy: Wonderdog Behavioral Training. You held me up to high standards and gave me incredible support, even in challenging times. You're a peach.

Toni Hage: Fun Dawgs Dog Training. I have watched you grow from a curious volunteer to an outstanding trainer and behaviorist—and an exceptional editor. Way to go, girl.

Marsha and Dale Quick: You are the most wonderful friends and neighbors a girl could ever have. What did you get me into? Hugs through the gate every single day.

Cari Rodman: You are always there, caring, and sharing my love for animals. Even with your own hurdles, you have supported me in every effort. You are *very* special to me.

To all the dogs (oh, come on, you knew that was coming) that have shared and influenced my life, from the German Shepherd Dog that bit me in the face when I was 6 years old, to my current side-kick, Twyla, a true terrier if I ever saw one.

Wait, there's more.

To anyone and everyone that looked at, used a red pen on, commented on, contemplated, folded, spindled and mutilated this work, thank you thank you thank you.

My nephew, **Dillon Green** - For our visit to the Union City Park Drigon Dog Park, thank you for your time and insights.

I put you, my partner and spouse, **Dannie O'Flaherty**, at the end because I can't easily express the love I have for you. Your tolerance of long hours at the computer without my washing any dishes, your stern encouragement to fight my frequent procrastination, and your warm feet in the middle of the night. You, DannieO, are "ma holy lub."

April 2009

photograph by Lucy Aron, Ragle Ranch Dog Park

MERCY
(May 31, 2009)

Just as I am finishing the final proof of
this book, we have lost our sweet 13-year-old
German Shepherd mix, **Mercy,** to illness.

We will sorely miss her love and
her silly triangle ears that touched
at the tips when she was listening
carefully. We will always smile as we
recall her intense wagging hunt for
the ball, and her thoughtful kindness
towards the world.

Table of Contents

For integration connections with GoogleEarth®, go to the website:
www.berrygrovedogs.com

Foreword

On a recent trip to British Columbia with our dog, my wife and I were delighted to observe a highway marker we'd never seen before: "Dog Park—Next Exit." Who could resist? It turned out the park was part of the Northwest Organization for Animal Help facility in Stanwood, Washington, where we spent a lovely hour or so meeting fellow vacationers. Over the rest of our time on the road, that exit sign got us to imagine others that would be points of interest for traveling dogs: "Squirrel Chasing Opportunities—Don't Miss It;" "No End of Things to Sniff—Ample Parking;" "Veterinary Hospital—Speed Up and Do Not Stop," and so on.

One of the goals of travel is to experience things that are important to us. Gourmets look forward to regional cuisines, art lovers to museums and galleries, outdoor recreationists to rivers and woods. Dog owners just as frequently want to know where the dog parks are, and for travelers in California, Gail S. Green has written the definitive guidebook. Organized by county and city, integrated with Google Earth®, and listing amenities from agility equipment to water availability, the book functions like a dog leading its reader to no end of treasures in at least 200 parks throughout the state.

In 1979, Gail was instrumental in establishing Ohlone Dog Park in Berkeley, CA, the nation's *first* bit of public land set aside by legal designation for dogs and their owners. That there are so many parks nowadays suggests that dog owners are appropriately seen as deserving their taxed slice of public resources. Dog parks, after all, are for people, just the same as tot lots and shuffleboard courts.

More or less every use of park space has its own human demographic, each getting folks out for some fresh air, conversation, and a feeling of community. Sometimes that experience overflows its boundaries: soccer moms get interested in child welfare matters; dog owners hold fundraisers for shelter animals; joggers race for a cure to AIDS … the list is as diverse as humankind. Love is like that, no matter its object; it connects us to the world by ever greater means.

Gail is such a person, and I cannot write about this book without thinking about her. It is easy to despair that the world has no shortage of ill will, and even worse sometimes that some that appear to do good works are disingenuous, wishing little more than to draw attention to themselves. Gail's activism in a broad spectrum of affairs—ranging from animal welfare to disaster relief to senior care—is selfless. She is wise, less enamored with the sound of her own voice than she is committed to do the hard work that must be done. She puts into words what deserves to be, and leaves the rest. This book is like her: a precious guide. Many think the same about their dogs. It is high praise.

Author Agnes Sligh Turnbull once observed: "Dog lives are too short. Their own fault, really." Few facts are so important to me. If you feel the same, purchase this book, hit the road, and give your dog a hug from Gail.

Paul Klein
Albany, California

photograph by Lucy Aron, Ragle Ranch Dog Park

Introduction

When I was in 6th grade, we had a "graduation" ceremony, and each of us in my class stood up and said what we wanted to do when we grew up. At my turn, I stood up and said: "I want to travel around in my motor home with my dog and write." Honest to goodness. I think, with this book, I have hit the mark.

It all started in February 2008. I sat on the sofa in my pajamas realizing I really hadn't declared a New Year's Resolution, and it was, frankly, getting late. Lose weight? Get more exercise? Stay in touch with friends and family more consistently? Stop smoking?

I never smoked.

What is my passion? I asked myself. Anything dogs, I answered myself. What do I love to do? I asked myself. Meet dog people, play with dogs, kiss dogs, work with dogs, get my knees dirty. Go to the dog park, I answered myself.

Many years ago, I was the co-founder of the first fenced dog park in the US. It was quite a chore, as many have found. Worth every moment in retrospect. Ohlone Dog Park in Berkeley, CA.

Wouldn't it be fun to visit other dog parks, ones that I have never been to? I would love to visit all the fenced dog parks in California! That would be such a fun little project, set a goal of one year. Wouldn't that be a kick!

I told Dannie about my idea, shrinking back a little at first waiting for the "Are you crazy, honey?" But it didn't happen that way. She lit up and said that it was a fun idea, and I should do it.

Then our friends, Marsha and Dale, got excited and said, "You could do a book!" I kicked the ground in front of me, thought for a moment, and said to myself, "Okay, this is getting out of hand." But I nodded and said "Yeah."

And so it began. The pure joy of the dogs, the respite of the travel, the places that were unbearably hot in the summer, the knee-deep snow in the winter and the hail knocking my hat off as I sloshed through puddles to talk to wonderful people. With little Twyla by my side for the adventure.

I have visited over 235 fenced dog parks from Redding to Chula Vista. It's been quite a trip. Here is the result of all that—muddy shoes and all.

"William"
photograph by Lucy Aron, Ragle Ranch Dog Park

Benefits of Dog Parks

Dog parks not only benefit dogs in many ways, but can also provide great advantage to the community.

Parks specifically designed and designated for dogs allow dogs to socialize, thereby contributing to future safety and comfort around new dogs as well as people.

Parks promote responsible pet ownership through peer education, and perhaps sometimes gentle peer pressure.

Parks enable dogs to run free, legally, in strictly enforced leash-law communities.

Parks support public health and safety by depositing feces and urine in areas that children (generally) do not play, and in so doing eliminate many concerns about zoonotic diseases on streets, in public areas and on private property. (Please remember to clean up after your dog – even in dog parks!)

Dogs that are exercised and socialized regularly tend to have fewer behavior problems in homes: boredom chewing, barking, anxiety and more. Anecdotal evidence suggests that communities supporting designated dog parks show a significant decrease in dogs given up to shelters and rescue groups for re-homing, thereby decreasing euthanasia numbers.

While my intention is to include as close to all of the fenced dog parks within the State of California as I can, new parks and park groups are being born almost daily.

My website may help you to locate new parks and negotiate old ones, get news, and join lecture or appearance locations:

www.berrygrovedogs.com

Play It Safe

The perfect dog park.

Don't look too hard—it doesn't exist. That doesn't mean we should not strive for it. Here you will find some of the common "do's" that I have found posted at the gates of many parks, plus a few of my own ideas to keep you and your dog safe while enjoying the benefits of a designated and fenced community dog park.

One of my biggest concerns is that many dog owners are unable to effectively read and understand the complexities of canine body language. It takes some reading, education and working with qualified trainers or behaviorists. It is time well spent.

Enroll your dog in an obedience class. You will learn much more than your dog, and it allows you to build a trusting and cohesive relationship. When you go to the dog park, you will have a responsive dog that others will "oooh" and "aaah" about, and ask you how you did that. You can then refer them to your wonderful trainer.

To call your dog to you, I suggest a unique whistle of some sort. I have a small train whistle for Twyla. It doesn't sound like a common whistle, and I don't have to embarrass myself trying the fingers-in-the-teeth thing. Her response is decent (she is a terrier, after all) with a belly-to-the-ground return to me, happy and leaping as she runs. She demonstrates this sort of recall because of the practice of "loading" the whistle. To "load" her whistle, I started with Twyla's "absolute-go-through-fire-for-it" treats. At home I blew the whistle immediately before offering her the treat. Soon she associated the whistle with that delicious favorite treat (and she never got that treat at any other time). We practiced at home in the same room, we practiced at home from different rooms, we practiced on leash walks, we practiced in outdoor enclosed areas, we practiced in an empty dog park. Three toots on the whistle keeps us connected in any environment. It is a safety net.

> **Another benefit of "loading" the
> whistle... in an emergency or
> natural disaster you may be
> separated from your dog.
> This familiar whistle may be
> your confused or frightened dog's
> lifeline back to you.**

So, here are some "do's" at the dog park in no particular order
(there are no "don'ts"—after all we are talking about positive
reinforcement training, yes?).

DO:

Have your dog spayed or neutered.

Watch your dog at all times.

Carry a leash.

Use a buckle collar (no pinch, prong, choke or other correction
collars—metal or fabric).

Have tags on your dog at all times.

Keep your dog on leash entering and exiting the park or staging
area.

Make sure your dog is at least 4 months old (I recommend even
older) and is up to date on all appropriate vaccinations. A full dog
park can be overwhelming for a young dog, and may leave a
negative impression for a long time. Little puppies need safe and
secure experiences to become well-adjusted adult dogs.

_DO:_

Wear shoes, for goodness sake.

Stay in the park with your dog during your entire visit.

Know the signs of illness or injury and take immediate action.

Know when to leave the park—if you OR your dog are uncomfort-able, it is time to go.

Be prepared to get dirty—not every dog has manners.

Avoid bringing small children (10 years old is a good cut off age), not all dogs like or understand children; even if your child "loves dogs," **it's not about the child**.

Avoid offering to take all of your neighbors' dogs to the park with you. Usually there is a 2-3 dog limit per person, and you may not REALLY know your neighbor's dog.

Keep your dog—big or little—on the ground unless safety becomes an immediate issue (if you must, scoop up your dog while you turn away from oncoming dogs).

Leave the treats for the dog, the snack for you and the cup of coffee in the car.

Be aware that dogs have different play styles. If your dog is over-whelmed by another dog's style, avoid arguing with other owners and take your dog and your pride out of the park.

Pick up poop—your dog's and another dog's for good measure.

Scope out the park before entering. If you are hesitant, take your dog for a walk, elsewhere. Trust your gut.

If your dog bites a person, report it to the local Police Department immediately. If your dog bites or injures another dog, do the right thing: get the dog and person to a veterinarian, and pay the bill.

DO:

Fill in any holes your dog digs. Even if he digs it up again.

Remember, your dog's behavior is not a reflection of you, but you must respond as though it is.

And finally: If using a tennis racket to lob the ball for your dog, look behind you before swinging.

photograph by Lucy Aron, Ragle Ranch Dog Park

"There are two rules
in our relationship with dogs:

1. The owner has to keep the dog safe;

2. The dog has to watch the owner."

- Trish King, CPDT, CDBC
Author: "Parenting Your Dog"
Director, Behavior and Training
Marin Humane Society

According to Twyla

As a trainer and behaviorist, I constantly remind clients (and irritated friends) not to anthropomorphize their animals; in other words, treat them like humans. But everyone does it at one time or another, even those of us seasoned in dog behavior.

If Twyla leapt into a park,
played, ran, jumped and panted,
found a small dog area and
disabled access (and if I did the same),
you will see this symbol:

If Twyla walked into a park,
sniffed and indicated this park
was good but found no small dog area
or disabled access (and if I did the same),
you will see this symbol:

If Twyla entered a park, stood there
looking baffled and turned to go
back to the gate (and if I did the same),
you will see this symbol:

Right, Twyla?
Twyla?
Honey, your mother is talking to you.

Alameda County

Alameda Dog Park

Eighth Street near
Central Avenue
(inside Washington Park)

These areas are hard to miss. Both the small dog area and the large dog areas are very well-attended and popular.

Well-policed by the users, there are few issues between the dogs most days. The small dog area is clean, while the area for the large dogs is not as clean if you walk the perimeter.

Very social group, regular events and get-togethers are provided that bring this community together for fun and education.

Amenities

Clean-up
Disabled access
Double-gated
Entrances: 3
Fenced
Grass/dirt
Parking
Restroom
Seating
Small dog area
Trees
Water

Concerns

Can be dusty or muddy

Many bushes in the large dog area block continuous sight of your dog

I have observed some owners leave dogs unattended

Local Veterinary Clinic

Providence Veterinary
Medical Group
Alameda

510-521-5775

Alameda Point Dog Run

Main Street,
west of Singleton Avenue

This area can provide a good run for large dogs or particularly active small dogs. Very open.

The park looks out on the Alameda Estuary, and sits next to the Alameda Ferry terminal.

When I was there Twyla and I were all alone, but the park appears to be well-used as evidenced by the many paw prints and skid marks in the dirt.

Lots of tennis balls...

Amenities

Clean-up
Disabled access
Double-gated
Entrances: 2
Fenced
Grass/dirt/chips
Parking
Seating
Trees
Water

Concerns

No small dog area

No restroom

Breezy, can be cold

Parking can be challenging during the week due to ferry parking

Local Veterinary Clinic

Providence Veterinary
Medical Group
Alameda

510-521-5775

Ohlone Dog Park

Hearst Street & Grant Street
(inside Ohlone Parkway)

This is the first designated fenced dog park in the United States.

It has a cement walkway that leads through the middle of the park from entrance to entrance, shaped like a dog bone in the center of the park.

There are some hay bales placed in potentially muddy areas, near water faucets and located where the park gets muddy in rain.

There are commemorative plaques to honor some important people in the park's history.

Very social and community-oriented.

Amenities

Bulletin board
Chips/dirt
Clean-up
Disabled access
Double-gated
Entrances: 2
Fenced
Seating
Street parking
Trees
Water

Concerns

Can be dusty

No small dog area

Use caution after dark

No restroom

Local Veterinary Clinic

Berkeley Dog and Cat Hospital
Berkeley

510-848-5041

Earl Warren Park

4660 Crow Canyon Road

This is a beautiful park and the surrounding area is very green with big oak trees.

Both large and small dog areas are very big. Hilly, sloped areas, but always easy to see your dog. Lots of seating.

Very popular park. Nice people, good sense of community. New users are welcomed openly.

No one in the small dog area when we visited—everyone mingled together nicely in the large dog area.

Amenities

Clean-up
Double-gated
Entrances: 2
Fenced
Grass/dirt
Parking
Restroom
Seating
Small dog area
Trees
Water

Concerns

Can be challenging to find—I ended up going in the back way

No disabled access

Local Veterinary Clinic

Castro Valley Veterinary Hospital
Castro Valley

510-582-3656

Dougherty Hills Dog Park

6575 Amador Valley Blvd.

The large dog area is a bit more interesting than the small dog area, but both are very nice. Clean and well-kept. Great drainage with river rocks from the water fountains to the outside of the park—very little mud.

A drawback I saw is that the large dog area has a small hill in the center, and you cannot always see your dog.

I especially like that the double-gated areas do not share a staging area. Hurray. Very nice park, I will visit again.

Amenities

Clean-up
Disabled access
Double-gated
Entrances: 2
Fenced
Grass/dirt
Parking
Play structure
Seating
Small dog area
Trees
Water

Concerns

It may be possible for small dogs to dig under the fence

Rattlesnake area

Can't always see your dog

No restroom

Local Veterinary Clinic

Dublin Veterinary Hospital
Dublin

925-828-5520

Central Park Dog Park

1110 Stevenson Blvd.

I had to hunt a little, because this park is way in the back of Central Park.

Unfortunately, there is no shade here and the area can be hot. Be careful where you walk—there are a lot of small holes to step in and you may twist an ankle.

It's too bad there's no small dog area as there is ample room to include one.

The people in the park were very pleasant and were gathered in small groups throughout the park. Twyla ran and ran with other small dogs.

Special Hours: Dawn-10 pm

Local Veterinary Clinic

Grimmer Blvd. Veterinary
Fremont

510-656-0223

Amenities

Bulletin board
Clean-up
Disabled access
Double-gated
Entrances: 1
Fenced
Grass/dirt
Parking
Seating
Water

Concerns

No shade

No small dog area

No restroom

Lake Elizabeth Dog Park

Stevenson Blvd.,
off of Paseo Padre

This park is located near the Tri-Valley shelter. There are rumors that the park may be moving, but no one is quite sure that I talked to.

Park is well-marked and easy to find. Has a nice informative bulletin board.

The people I met here were extremely nice and appear to be a good and caring community.

The biggest concern is that there is really no shade provided.

Amenities

Bulletin board
Clean-up
Disabled access
Double-gated
Entrances: 1
Fenced
Grass/dirt/chips
Parking
Restroom
Seating
Trees
Water

Concerns

No shade

Can be extremely hot on warm days

No small dog area

Local Veterinary Clinic

Grimmer Blvd. Veterinary
Fremont

510-656-0223

Bruno Canziana Neighborhood Park

South Charlotte Way,
Two Blocks East of East Avenue

This is an open lawn area, great for a good hard dog run and romp, but that's about it. The park is extremely clean and green, but with the openness, it has no protection from rain or heat.

When I was there, there were three young dogs racing and chasing, having a great time—no cares about seating or disabled access, just all out speed. They think this is a wonderful area!

The community is terrific—very much a close-knit group during my visit. I felt an instant member of the group.

On a mild day this is a beautiful area. If there were a small dog area, I might bring Twyla with me.

Local Veterinary Clinic

Livermore Veterinary Hospital
Livermore

925-447-1420

Amenities

Clean-up
Entrances: 3
Fenced
Grass
Parking

Concerns

No small dog area

No disabled access

No seating

Flooding

No double gates

Water is outside of the park

Marlin A. Pound Neighborhood Park

2010 Bluebell Drive

Some call this "Springtown Dog Park," and this park is terrific. Lots of shade—Livermore can get quite warm. Trees abound, but I was concerned that the roots are so exposed that a running dog could catch a foot and get injured.

One great feature—in the large dog area, the picnic table surfaces extend out the end of the table farther than the benches, providing a shaded area for large dogs that can't fit under foot at the tables. Brilliant!

I loved this park, and wish I lived closer! No one was there so I didn't get a feel for the community, but the park is wonderful.

Amenities

Clean-up
Disabled access
Double-gated
Entrances: 3
Fenced
Grass/asphalt
Seating
Small dog area
Trees
Water

Local Veterinary Clinic

Livermore Veterinary Hospital
Livermore

925-447-1420

Concerns

Lots of open tree roots

Water in joined staging area

Located at very far end of the park

Max Baer Dog Park

Murdell Lane between
Stanley Blvd & Concannon

This is a beautiful park. Green and lush. Trees are abundant and provide wonderful shade.

The surface of this park is nice and flat—great for a good run.

One of the best things about this visit was the demonstration of good owner control of their dogs. No inappropriate behavior (by dogs, or people) was tolerated, and the park-goers were social and welcoming.

Toys, balls and tennis rackets abound.

Amenities

Clean-up
Disabled access
Double-gated
Entrances: 1
Fenced
Grass/dirt
Parking
Seating
Trees
Water

Concerns

No small dog area

No restroom

Local Veterinary Clinic

Livermore Veterinary Hospital
Livermore

925-447-1420

May Nissen Dog Park

685 Rincon Avenue

This park is small but nice. It doesn't have a lot of character and is not impressive, but if you're a dog, you don't care. It's a great park for a dog that's been cooped up all day...

I was warned about being in this park after dark, just that there are a few questionable regulars. However, no one could mention any particular incident.

Twyla had a good run with other small dogs, and I recommend this park for the average pup.

Amenities

Clean-up
Double-gated
Entrances: 2
Fenced
Grass/dirt
Lights
Parking
Restroom
Seating
Trees
Water

Concerns

No small dog area

Be cautious after dark

No disabled access

Local Veterinary Clinic

Livermore Veterinary Hospital
Livermore

925-447-1420

Vista Meadows Park

Westminster & Lambeth Road

This park is up the grassy hill past the playground—you cannot see it from the street. And the grassy hill is not an easy trek. Did I miss another entrance?

Once in the park, it has rolling hills and grass to run and play on. This is a popular park. Very social atmosphere, and everyone seems to know everyone else!

Nice views from this park.

Amenities

Clean-up
Double-gated
Entrances: 1
Fenced
Grass/Dirt
Street parking
Seating
Trees
Water

Concerns

No small dog area

No restroom

No disabled access

Local Veterinary Clinic

Livermore Veterinary Hospital
Livermore

925-447-1420

Hardy Dog Park

491 Hardy and Claremont

This park is fairly barren, but it's quite popular. The down side is this park is under a noisy freeway overpass while the upside is that this park is under a freeway overpass and stays dry in rainy weather and cool on hot days.

The community is quite strong here, social and the park is often quite busy. People are welcoming in this park.

The water area is often pretty muddy, but the rest of the surface is hard dirt and chips.

We come by this park whenever we are in the area.

Amenities

Bulletin board
Clean-up
Dirt/chips
Disabled access
Double-gated
Entrances: 2
Fenced
Restroom
Seating
Trees
Water

Concerns

No small dog area

Noisy—under the freeway

Local Veterinary Clinic

Broadway Pet Hospital
Oakland

510-653-0212

Joaquin Miller Dog Park / Gizmoland

Sanborn off Joaquin Miller Blvd.
(inside Joaquin Miller Park)

This is in a large regional park in the hills of Oakland. The large park has multiple acres with picnic areas, and amphitheater, and miles of paths and hiking.

Tall beautiful trees on the outside perimeter of both park areas. Seating is provided by large logs lining the fences.

Very active community involved with the Oakland dog parks. People in the park appear to be very responsible for their dog's behavior.

Special meet-ups occur occasionally.

Amenities

Chips
Clean-up
Double-gated
Entrances: 2
Fenced
Parking
Restroom
Seating
Small dog area
Telephone
Trees
Water

Concerns

No disabled access

Not always available for dogs—used for special park event parking

Chips in the park can be hard on dog feet

Local Veterinary Clinic

Skyline Veterinary Hospital
Oakland

510-531-8280

Mosswood Park Dog Park

Webster Street & 36th Street
(inside Mosswood Park)

It is clearly posted that this park does not allow prong or pinch collars, and dogs that enter the park must be micro-chipped.

The large and small dog areas are separated by the parking lot. The requirements on dog size are posted on large signs.

Very shady and cool park. Great community involvement and support. Both sides of the park have good running area. Located behind the tennis courts.

Amenities

Asphalt/dirt
Clean-up
Disabled access
Double-gated
Entrances: 2
Fenced
Parking
Restroom
Seating
Small dog area
Trees

Concerns

Flooding problems in the rain

May not be a safe area to be in after dark

No water

Local Veterinary Clinic

Broadway Pet Hospital
Oakland

510-653-0212

Muirwood Dog Park

4701 Muirwood Drive
(inside Muirwood Park)

The dog area is at the back of this grassy park.

This is a nice park, but the small dog area is too small. The park areas are very green and lush, clean. Lots of trees and shade both inside and outside the parks.

Long but not very wide dog run area. The people are very sociable and friendly, and were very welcoming.

Nice park but note the concerns below.

Amenities

Chips
Clean-up
Double-gated
Entrances: 2
Fenced
Parking
Seating
Small dog area
Trees
Water

Concerns

Wood chips are vey large—hard on small dog feet

Park is next to freeway with sound wall, but noisy

No restroom

No disabled access

Local Veterinary Clinic

Pleasanton Veterinary Hospital
Pleasanton

925-462-7750

San Lorenzo Dog Park

1970 Via Buena Vista
(inside San Lorenzo
Community Park)

The first time I visited this park it was a little challenging to find.

The small dog area is pretty barren and very small. Very little shade.

The pond in the area is beautiful.

The other dog owners were very warm and welcoming. Twyla made a small Maltese puppy friend and appeared to have a lots of fun.

Amenities

Clean-up
Dirt/Grass
Disabled access
Double-gated
Entrances: 2
Fenced
Parking
Restroom
Seating
Small dog area
Trees
Water

Concerns

Small dog area has no amenities at all

Local Veterinary Clinic

San Lorenzo Veterinary Hospital
San Lorenzo

510-276-7234

Drigon Dog Park

7th Street @ Mission Blvd.

_____

This park is beautifully landscaped and well-groomed. There is an agility course all around the inside perimeter of the large dog park, as well as small agility equipment inside the small dog area.

Cement fire hydrants are placed throughout the park. (If you looked at the park from an aerial view, you would see it is shaped like a dog bone.)

Great community of people, friendly and helpful to newcomers. Great exercise area for running. And with new solar lights!

Special Hours: Closed Mondays

Local Veterinary Clinic

Veterinary Medical Center
Union City

510-441-8500

Amenities

Agility equipment
Asphalt/dirt/grass
Clean-up
Disabled access
Double-gated
Entrances: 2
Fenced
SOLAR Lights
Seating
Shade structure
Small dog area
Trees
Water

Concerns

Can be hot, limited shade

No restroom

Small dog area is quite small

Butte County

DeGarmo Dog Park

Leora Court & The Esplanade

While I was unable to visit this park, I did get some information and thoughts of users.

One of the main comments is that the park is pretty small, and can get overly crowded at high times of the day or week. There were also references to the park not being as clean as some, that owners are not diligent about cleaning up after their dogs.

But most folks are very happy to have this park here, and use it regularly. I will be visiting it soon and can give my own review on my website.

Amenities

Clean-up
Disabled access
Fenced
Grass
Lights
Seating
Wading pool
Water

Concerns

No small dog area

Small park

Local Veterinary Clinic

Chico Animal Hospital
Chico

530-342-0518

Contra Costa County

Clayton Dog Park

Marsh Creek Road and
Regency Drive

This park is set back in a larger park area, and has a long slender pathway on a slope to the entrance, off of Regency. Can be risky when passing dogs to and from the park unless you have good control of your dog, and so does the other owner.

Was not very busy the few times we have been there.

This was not one of my favorites, but if you need a dog park and live in the area, it fills the need to run.

Amenities

Clean-up
Chips
Disabled access
Fenced
Seating

Concerns

No water provided

No restroom

No small dog area

Local Veterinary Clinic

Alpine Veterinary Hospital
Concord

925-825-8464

The Paw Patch Dog Park

Ayers and Turtle Creek
(inside Newhall Park)

Great park, another favorite. Nicely groomed—the park is fenced off in areas when the grass needs re-seeding, lots of room to run in large dog area, very appropriate size for running in the small dog area.

The community here is very social and friendly. The group tends to police the park well and owners with aggressive dogs are pressured out of the park immediately.

Toy box has lots of balls and Frisbees. I like this park a lot.

Special Hours: Closed Wednesdays

Local Veterinary Clinic

Alpine Veterinary Hospital
Concord

925-825-8464

Amenities

Clean-up
Disabled access
Double-gated
Entrances: 1
Fenced
Grass/dirt
Parking
Restroom
Seating
Small dog area
Trees
Water

Concerns

Small dogs can escape the area under the gate and get into the large dog area

Can be hot, very little shade

Canine Corral Dog Park

1029 La Gonda Way
(inside Hap Magee Ranch)

This is a great park. The larger park is a multi-use park that is wonderfully maintained. A lot of families use this area, but no children were in the dog area.

A lot of young trees within the dog areas will be very shady when grown.

The people and the dogs using this park were friendly and warm. Appear to have good control of the dogs, with people taking appropriate and timely responsibility for their dogs. One of my favorites!

Amenities

Clean-up
Disabled access
Double-gated
Entrances: 2
Fenced
Grass/chips
Parking
Restroom
Seating
Small dog area
Trees
Water

Concerns

Rattlesnake area

Local Veterinary Clinic

Bishop Ranch Veterinary Center
San Ramon

925-866-8387

Point Isabel Regional Park

Isabel Road,
at end Central Avenue

This is dog-heaven. Only partially fenced, but I couldn't leave this one out. A long asphalt path leads next to the Bay inlet, where swimming is customary. A bridge at the end of the park leads to another large area. You can take a nice long brisk walk with your dog as it engages with other dogs.

Mudpuppy's Tub & Scrub provides a dog bath and some supplies right there inside the park. There is the Sit & Stay Café, where you can get the best hot cocoa in the state for those chilly morning walks.

Have some fun!

Pt. Isabel is the happenin' place.

Amenities

Bulletin boards
Clean-up
Disabled access
Fenced—Partial
Grass/dirt/asphalt
Parking
Restroom
Seating
Water

Concerns

Dogs can get out
of owner's sight

Partially fenced

Café serves food
accessible to dogs
that are unleashed

Mud and foxtails

Must keep dogs
out of wildlife area

No small dog area

Local Veterinary Clinic

Codornices Veterinary Clinic
Albany

510-524-3062

Pinole Valley Dog Park

Pinole Valley Blvd. & Simas
(inside Pinole Valley Park)

This is another favorite. The small dog area used to have a big tree in the middle, providing great shade, but it apparently died and had to be removed. It's still a great stump to lift legs on.

Seating is in the shade. People are friendly and warm, and interested in each other's dogs. The regulars appear to be very supportive of each other, and were quite welcoming to newcomers.

Take layers to wear, it can get cool in the morning and late afternoon.

Amenities

Clean-up
Double-gated
Entrances: 3
Fenced
Grass/dirt/chips
Parking
Restroom
Seating
Small dog area
Trees
Water

Concerns

Can be muddy

No disabled access

Some owners lack control of their big dogs

Lots of gophers

Local Veterinary Clinic

Pinole Pet Hospital
Pinole

510-724-8766

Paso Nogal Dog Park

Paso Nogal Road,
west of Morello Avenue

This park has seen lots of changes, and it appears to be improving each time I go. This is another fave.

I did witness several people letting their dogs into the park and then sitting in their cars—a dangerous way to give the dogs some exercise.

All the people were very welcoming and social. The large dog area gives lots of running room, but the small dog area could be a touch larger.

Again, I like this park.

Amenities

Clean-up
Disabled access
Double-gated
Entrances: 2
Fenced
Grass/dirt
Parking
Seating
Small dog area
Trees
Water

Concerns

Small dog area does not have it's own water—has to be bucketed in from large dog area

No restroom

Local Veterinary Clinic

Sun Valley Animal Hospital
Pleasant Hill

925-686-6363

Bollinger Dog Park

Bollinger Canyon,
west of San Ramon Valley Blvd.
(inside Memorial Park)

This is a nice park, although it was very hot the day we were there. There is a shade structure with seating, but no trees.

The people that attend the park were very warm and friendly, and seemed to take appropriate responsibility for their dogs. As a result, the park was very clean and well-groomed.

The small dog area was not in use when we were visiting. All the dogs, large and small, were in the large dog area, which can be risky for the small dogs. I liked this park quite a bit.

Amenities

Bulletin board
Clean-up
Dirt/gravel
Disabled access
Double-gated
Entrances: 2
Fenced
Parking
Restroom
Seating
Shade structure
Small dog area
Water

Concerns

Can be very hot

Gravel can be tough on paws of dogs running and skidding to a stop

Local Veterinary Clinic

San Ramon Veterinary Hospital
San Ramon

925-837-0526

Del Mar Dog Park

Del Mar & Pine Valley Road

This is a relatively compact park with no small dog area. The P G & E transformers in the middle of the park make it very disjointed, as do the many bushes in the park. The chips are large and hard to walk on. Twyla had a very tough time walking in this park.

The park is oddly arranged, and I found it difficult at first to see if there were other dogs in the park—this can be quite unsafe.

The people at this park, when I found them, were isolated and not interested in socializing. Not my favorite park.

Local Veterinary Clinic

San Ramon Veterinary Hospital
San Ramon

925-837-0526

Amenities

Chips
Clean-up
Double-gated
Entrances: 2
Fenced
Trees
Seating
Shade structure
Water

Concerns

No restroom

No small dog area

Chips are very large and difficult to walk on

Bushes make it easy to lose sight of your dog

No disabled access

Wag World Dog Park—Heather Farm

301 N. San Carlos Drive
(inside Heather Farms Park)

This is a wonderful park. Very busy, it has been full of activity during every visit I have made. One of my faves!

Well-groomed and maintained, very green and inviting. The trees in the small dog area provide lots of shade in the heat, but the seating is not near the trees. An asphalt walkway runs throughout the park, so accessibility is great.

The people in this park were very social and friendly. I really like this park!

Amenities

Clean-up
Disabled access
Double-gated
Entrances: 2
Fenced
Parking
Grass/asphalt
Restroom
Seating
Small dog area
Trees
Water

Concerns

One staging area for both parks

Water located in staging area so must be taken into parks in bowls or buckets

Local Veterinary Clinic

Ygnacio Animal Hospital
Walnut Creek

925-935-4880

Fresno County

El Capitan Dog Park

4257 W. Alamos

This was Fresno's first dog park. It is located in an industrial area within the city. The park is hilly, with several trees surrounding the perimeter. It can be extremely muddy and squishy after a rain.

During our visit, there was only one other person and dog, but the weather was cold and that could explain it.

The person I met said the park was well-used, and no one really paid attention to the closing sign.

Special Hours: 6 am-10 pm, April through December

Local Veterinary Clinic

Adobe Animal Hospital
Fresno

559-439-1510

Amenities

Bulletin board
Clean-up
Disabled access
Double-gated
Entrances: 1
Fenced
Grass/asphalt
Lights
Parking
Seating
Trees
Wading pools
Water

Concerns

Flooding problems

Sewer access in mid-park, with fence around it

No restroom

No small dog area

Woodward Park Dog Park

Friant & East Auburn Drive
(inside Woodward Park)

Woodward Park is a very large park—
several miles in range. The dog area is
approximately one mile in from the
main gate.

Can be very warm on hot days. Lots of
trees and shade. Lots and lots of tennis
balls! Good mix of dogs when we
visited, people were attentive and
responsible with their dogs.

Friendly people, very welcoming. This
is a wonderful park. I'll be back.

Special Hours: 9 am-10 pm

Amenities

Bulletin board
Clean-up
Disabled access
Double-gated
Entrances: 1
Fee: $3.00
Fenced
Grass/dirt/chips
Parking
Restroom
Seating
Trees
Water

Local Veterinary Clinic

Adobe Animal Hospital
Fresno

559-439-1510

Concerns

No small dog area

Kern County

Centennial Dog Park

Montclair Street & Marella Way
(inside Centennial Park)

This park is located in a sump area, as are most of the Bakersfield dog areas. They are all often closed after severe weather due to flooding.

This was a large, relatively plain, park area with nothing exciting about it. However, it is quite popular and used all the time.

Very nice people at this park, very welcoming and friendly. Twyla met and showed a lot of interest in a little Maltese pup with whom she ran and leaped and ran.

Amenities

Clean-up
Double-gated
Entrances: 2
Fenced
Grass
Parking
Restrooms
Trees
Water

Concerns

Flooding issues

No disabled access

Few amenities

No small dog area

The park is challenging to find

Local Veterinary Clinic

Bakersfield Veterinary Hospital
Bakersfield

661-327-4444

Kroll Dog Park

Kroll Way & Montalvo Drive
(inside Kroll Park)

This park, like most in the Bakersfield area, is in a sump area. Can get very muddy and flooded in severe weather. One area in the park was a muddy puddle, and there were several pleas from dog owners trying to get their dogs out of the mud, all of it followed by laughter—very muddy pups!

The people at this park were exceptionally nice. I sat and talked for a very long time (while always watching Twyla!).

Trees were young when we visited and did not provide much shade.

Amenities

Clean-up
Entrances: 2
Fenced
Grass
Parking
Restroom
Seating
Trees
Water

Concerns

No small dog area

No disabled access

Flooding issues

Water outside gate

Local Veterinary Clinic

Bakersfield Veterinary Hospital
Bakersfield

661-327-4444

Season's Park Small Dog Area

Harris near Gosford
(in Silver Creek District)

This is the definition of a "small dog area." It is tiny, with one table/bench, and no water. The trees do provide nice shade, however.

No large dogs are allowed in this park, and I can see why—they wouldn't fit.

In the middle of a beautiful area and neighborhood, and the people that I met were very nice. It was quite hot, though, and Twyla walked into the park, found some shade and fell into a deep sleep. Had there been a big chair, I would have done the same.

Amenities

Clean-up
Double-gated
Entrances: 1
Fenced
Grass
Seating
Small dog area
Trees

Concerns

No large dog area

No water

Extremely small

No restroom

No disabled access

Local Veterinary Clinic

Bakersfield Veterinary Hospital
Bakersfield

661-327-4444

University Park Dog Area

University Avenue between
Camden and Mission Hills

This park is located in a sump area, as are many of Bakersfield parks, so flooding occurs in the rain and then the park is closed. The park used to be a soccer field but the flooding became a problem. So it was turned into a dog run area, and the neighbors seem to be pleased to have a place their dogs can stretch out.

The welcome was warm in this park, and Twyla gained another fan—a little Maltese puppy named Ziggy, that followed her everywhere she went in the park. I would like to see a tree or two inside this park. I did enjoy our time at this park.

Amenities

Clean-up
Double-gated
Entrances: 2
Fenced
Grass
Parking
Seating

Concerns

Flooding

No shade

No water other than what visitors carried in

No restroom

No disabled access

No small dog area

Local Veterinary Clinic

Bakersfield Veterinary Hospital
Bakersfield

661-327-4444

Wilson Dog Park

Wilson Road & Hughes Lane

This park is located in a sunken sump area, as are several dog areas in Bakersfield. It is closed in the rainy season because it floods.

It is a large park where a big Yellow Labrador came running full speed to greet us when we entered. Twyla gets very silly with Labs and Goldens, and she greeted him with leaps and freezes.

There's not much to say about this park, other than it's big and green and can be muddy. I would have liked to see more shade, given the area.

Amenities

Clean-up
Double-gated
Entrances: 2
Fenced
Grass
Parking
Restroom
Trees

Concerns

Flooding

Trees outside fenced area

No small dog area

No water

No disabled access

Multi-use park— soccer field

Local Veterinary Clinic

Bakersfield Veterinary Hospital
Bakersfield

661-327-4444

Meadowbrook Dog Park

Westwood Blvd. & Red Apple

Opened in September 2008, this park is in a beautiful setting in the high desert, and was covered in snow when I was there. Dogs had to leap to get from one end to another and as I always say "a tired dog is a good dog."

This wonderful park is well-arranged, very social with a great community. Started by the owners of Canine Creek Pet Wash and Boutique, in Tehachapi, there has been much forethought put into the design and care, and this park is clearly well-used. I am anxious to visit here again! Another wonderful favorite.

Amenities

Bulletin board
Clean-up
Double-gated
Entrances: 2
Fenced
Grass/dirt/chips
Parking
Seating
Small dog area
Restroom
Trees
Water

(This park is still in process—more amenities are planned! Disabled access pending?)

Local Veterinary Clinic

Antelope Valley
Veterinary Hospital
Palmdale

661-273-1234

Concerns

No disabled access

Kings County

Freedom Park

Grangeville on 9 1/4 Street

This park was a welcome addition to the small town of Hanford. However, it leaves a lot of room for improvement, and appears to still be under construction.

Very barren and small. Small dog area is extremely small, large dog area is bigger and longer with a good area for the larger dogs to run.

This park is part of a larger family park. I will return as it improves.

Amenities

Clean-up
Disabled access
Double-gated
Entrances: 1
Fenced
Grass
Parking
Restroom
Seating
Small dog area
Water

Concerns

No shade at all

Can get very hot

Challenging to find

Local Veterinary Clinic

Hanford Veterinary Hospital, Inc.
Hanford

559-584-4481

Los Angeles County

Eisenhower Memorial Dog Park

601 N. 2nd Avenue

One of my favorites! A sweet park, with disabled access throughout the entire park. To get to the dog areas, I crossed a wonderful covered wooden bridge over a big wash area.

Both large and small dog areas were full of interrupters, trees and tables. However, there is some flooding in the rain. Beautiful big shady trees, very warm and inviting. I was alone when I visited. It was raining quite hard; but being a die-hard dog park person, it didn't dampen my enthusiasm.

I will be back!

Special Hours: Closed Thursdays before 11 am

Local Veterinary Clinic

Arcadia Small Animal Hospital
Arcadia

626-447-2244

Amenities

Bulletin board
Clean-up
Disabled access
Double-gated
Entrances: 4
Fenced
Grass/dirt/asphalt
Restroom
Seating
Small dog area
Trees
Water

Concerns

Flooding

A short sound-wall lines one side of the park, but I can't imagine it protects the neighbors from barking noise

Barrington Dog Park

333 S. Barrington Avenue

Very shady, this park is ideal on hot days. It also provides some protection from the rain, although the mud is a problem near the fountain. The park has several sections (I believe I counted 4-5?) and during my visit some of them were closed for maintenance while others remained open. There is a parking lot dividing all of the areas. It seemed some of the users weren't sure what was where, either.

Huge area, great for good long runs, with lots of interesting trees. Nice community and very welcoming.

Special Hours: Closed Tuesday AM

Amenities

Bulletin board
Clean-up
Disabled access
Double-gated
Entrances: 5
Fenced
Grass/dirt/chips
Parking
Restroom
Seating
Small dog area
Trees
Water

Concerns

Flooding

Can be tricky to determine which part is for which size dog—tiny small, medium small and large dog areas

Local Veterinary Clinic

Brent-Air Animal Hospital
Brentwood

310-478-0011

Calabasas Bark Park

4232 Las Virgines Road

This is a lovely park, with both large and small dog areas and a third area that is fenced and has limited hours. The small and large dog areas have a gate between them that can be opened up to create one larger area.

There is a nice community of people that use this park, a regular meeting every evening, as happens at many dog parks. Friends are made, and dogs become accustomed to playing with favorite pooches. Clean and very comfortable. I will be back.

Special Hours: 5 am-9 pm

Amenities

Clean-up
Double-gated
Entrances: 2
Fenced
Dirt/chips
Lights
Parking
Restroom
Seating
Shade structure
Small dog area
Trees
Water

Local Veterinary Clinic

Animal Emergency Care Center
Calabasas

818-880-0888

Concerns

No disabled access

Rattlesnake area

Claremont Pooch Park

100 S. College Avenue

This is a WONDERFUL park, full of fun interrupters, and amenities galore. The landscaping is gorgeous, and the park is interesting to walk through as well. The people that use this park were friendly, warm, welcoming and quite involved in the park's care and maintenance. Shady trees are in both large and small areas, with plenty of seating.

My only real concern was that the fence is only three feet high. I will be back! A fave. Can I have more than 10 in my top 10?

Hours: 6 am-10 pm, Closed Fridays 10-11:30 am

Amenities

Bulletin board
Clean-up
Disabled access
Double-gated
Entrances: 2
Fenced
Grass/dirt/gravel
Lights
Parking
Restroom
Seating
Shade structure
Small dog area
Trees
Water

Local Veterinary Clinic

Inland Animal Hospital
Ontario

909-947-4040

Concerns

The fence is only 3 feet tall

The Boneyard

Duquesne Avenue & Jefferson

This is a classy park. The entrance is under a blue trellis with the name of the park printed on it. There is a shared staging area before the double-gated areas for each park entrance.

Very nice people, all very friendly to each other. Nice community. Very involved in their park, keeping it clean and well groomed.

One of my favorite aspects, a sign on the small "time-out" area: "15 minute limit—if you need more time, it's time to go home."

Amenities

Bulletin board
Clean-up
Disabled access
Double-gated
Entrances: 2
Fenced
Gravel
Parking
Seating
Shade structure
Small dog area
Time-out area
Water

Concerns

Rattlesnake area

Shared staging

No restroom

No trees

Local Veterinary Clinic

City of Angels
Veterinary Specialty Center
Culver City

310-558-6111

El Segundo Dog Park

600 E. Imperial Avenue

This is a favorite. Both large and small dog areas are big, with lots of room to play and stretch out. There were several pine trees providing great weather protection.

The community and neighborhood are strongly supportive of this park, and if any problems occur, the police are very responsive and helpful.

The people at this park were quite wonderful and very eager to talk about their park and the community support.

Twyla and I will definitely be back!

Amenities

Bulletin boards
Clean-up
Double-gated
Entrances: 2
Fenced
Grass/dirt
Seating
Small dog area
Trees
Water

Local Veterinary Clinic

Animal Medical Group
Manhattan Beach

310-546-5731

Concerns

No disabled access

No restroom

Sepulveda Basin Off-leash Park

17550 Victory Blvd.

HUGE park! There are three areas here, all divided by a parking lot. Large dog, small dog, and a common area (where dogs of all sizes are allowed together). There were some closed areas due to grass re-seeding.

There are very loyal attendees, I was told, that frequent the park and sponsor vaccination and health clinics on some Sundays.

When I visited it was dusk and a bit chilly, but the numerous old trees appear to give lots of shade and wet weather protection. I really liked this park, and rate it a top 10.

Special Hours: Closed Friday AM

Local Veterinary Clinic

Encino Veterinary Clinic
Encino

818-783-7387

Amenities

Bulletin boards
Clean-up
Disabled access
Entrances: 6
Fenced
Grass/dirt
Restroom
Seating
Small dog area
Trees
Water

Concerns

No double-gate

Forrest E. Hull Dog Park

30th Street and L-12 Avenue

A dream come true on a hot day--there's a soda machine! When I was there the ground was covered with small bits of snow, which the dogs were sliding on and eating. Everyone was bundled up and laughing, and folks were welcoming as I entered.

This is one of the most popular parks in the area—wait, it's also currently the ONLY dog park in the area. It is located in a newly developed housing area in the high desert. The small and large dog areas provide lots of running room, and the snow made it great fun. I liked the park as well as the community. I'd love to return here.

Hours: 6 am-10 pm, Closed on Thursday 12 noon—3 pm

Local Veterinary Clinic

Smith Veterinary Hospital
Lancaster

661-948-5065

Amenities

Clean-up
Disabled access
Double-gated
Entrances: 5
Fenced
Grass/dirt
Lights
Parking
Restroom
Seating
Small dog area
Trees
Water

Concerns

Flooding

Rattlesnake area

Long Beach Recreation Dog Park

5201 E. 7th Street

This was a really fun park—with lots of beautiful eucalyptus trees, big old stumps, fallen trees and bus-stop benches everywhere, not to mention a huge mound of dirt in the middle of the park.

This is the park that was used in filming the movie "Must Love Dogs" and the users are quite proud of this fact. The social group was warm and welcoming. There is frequently no one in the small dog area and they all congregate in the big dog area. Twyla had great fun with two little dogs on Thanksgiving Day. We'll surely return. One of my faves!

Special Hours: Dawn-10 pm, Closed Monday AM

Local Veterinary Clinic

Blue Cross Veterinary Hospital
Signal Hill

562-494-0975

Amenities

Bulletin board
Clean-up
Disabled access
Double-gated
Entrances: 3
Fenced
Dirt/gravel
Lights
Parking
Play structures
Restroom
Seating
Small dog area
Trees
Water

Concerns

The small dog area is not as clean and well kept up as the large dog area— smelled of urine

Griffith Park Dog Park

Dead end of North Zoo Drive,
next to John Ferrar Soccer Field

This lovely park used to be a storage area for the Department of Water and Power. While the ground is mostly hard dirt, and there is some complaint about the mud, it is filled with large old trees, and a welcoming community.

As I was talking to folks at the tables, a huge Red-nose Pit Bull named Chico slowly climbed the table, ambled over and sat right in front of my face. He then planted a big wet slurp on my nose. How could you not love a park when Chico's around?

A relaxing visit, and I'd love to return when I get back in the area. Nice park.

Special Hours: 6 am—10 pm

Local Veterinary Clinic

Best Friends Animal Hospital
North Hollywood

818-766-2140
818-984-2698

Amenities

Bulletin board
Clean-up
Disabled access
Double-gated
Entrances: 2
Fenced
Grass/dirt
Parking
Restroom
Seating
Small dog area
Trees
Water

Concerns

Flooding

Hermon Dog Park

5568 Via Marisol
(inside Arroyo Seco Park)

This is a charming park with lots of personality. The park is flat with some trees. It is, as are many, a park in progress. The people involved were quite active in the evolution of this area.

Attendees are quite diverse—people and dogs—and there is a local trainer who teaches classes near the dog park so lots of well-behaved dogs frequent here. I had a good time, met with one of the founders and stayed quite a long while. I easily recommend this park, and I'll be back!

Amenities

Bulletin board
Clean-up
Disabled access
Double-gated
Entrances: 2
Fenced
Grass/gravel
Parking
Restroom
Seating
Small dog area
Trees
Water

Concerns

Rattlesnake area

Tricky to find—beyond the grassy area and under the overpass at the far end of the park

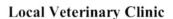

Local Veterinary Clinic

Center Sinai Animal Hospital
Los Angeles

310-559-3770

Silver Lake Dog Park

1850 Silverlake Blvd.

This park was rated highly by a national dog food company, but I looked diligently for the reason. It is quite barren, and on a significant slope so all the rain water creates long "streams" and ditches down the slope and dumps water directly into the small dog area. The "streams" are deep and could easily injure a person's ankle or a dog's foot.

During our visit it was quite busy with several dog scuffles. I suppose this park is fine if you live in the area, but I wouldn't travel any distance.

Hours: 6 am-10 pm, closed Tuesdays and Fridays 6-8:30 am

Amenities

Bulletin board
Clean-up
Double-gated
Entrances: 3
Fenced
Dirt
Seating
Shade structure
Small dog area
Trees
Water

Concerns

Flooding

No restrooms

No disabled access

Local Veterinary Clinic

Center Sinai Animal Hospital
Los Angeles

310-559-3770

Whitnall Dog Park

5801 1/2 Whitnall Highway

This is the perfect example of a park that has little-to-no-charm whatsoever, and is one of the best parks I visited. It is basic, grubby, junky and dirty. The community of people is fantastic. A great group!

Apparently this community hosts several events a year that benefit the neighborhood animals and residents. There are shot clinics, a spay/neuter van, and educational events.

At first sight I didn't like this park at all, but hearing all the good things changed my mind quickly. We'll be back for sure.

Amenities

Clean-up
Disabled access
Double-gated
Entrances: 4
Fenced
Grass/dirt
Restroom
Seating
Small dog area
Trees
Water

Concerns

Busy street

Flooding

Industrial area—lots of trucks

Local Veterinary Clinic

Best Friends Animal Hospital
North Hollywood

818-766-2140
818-984-2698

Alice's Off-leash Dog Park

3026 E. Orange Grove Blvd.
(Alice Frost Kennedy Off-leash)

When I was there, it was raining cats and cats, and began to hail as soon as I got out of the car. One young dog began to run and catch the hail. I have to say these are dedicated dog owners!

There is some disabled access, but if one had limited mobility one could not escape the weather at all. No cover in that area.

I liked this park a lot. The weekday crowds are quite supportive and provide a friendly community. There are regulars, as in many parks, the morning shift and the afternoon shift. I will be back—great park.

Amenities

Bulletin board
Clean-up
Disabled access
Double-gated
Entrances: 3
Fenced
Grass/dirt/asphalt
Parking
Restroom
Seating
Shade structure
Small dog area
Trees
Water

Concerns

Flooding

Very few shade areas

Local Veterinary Clinic

Foothill Veterinary Hospital
Pasadena

626-792-1187

Redondo Beach Dog Park

200 Flagler Lane
(next to Dominquez Park)

This is a nice park. I liked that the surface is varied (grass, dirt, chips and gravel) and was pretty easy on the feet and paws.

Two of the three areas are quite large, with a third area that is a bit smaller. There was no indication what the third area was used for, but generally extra areas are used for shy or aggressive or disabled/elderly dogs.

Great community of people, a lot of folks and dogs when we were there. A very active dog park group!

Special Hours: Closed Wednesday AM

Local Veterinary Clinic

Animal Hospital of Redondo Beach
Redondo Beach

310-540-9044

Amenities

Bulletin board
Clean-up
Disabled access
Double-gated
Entrances: 2
Fenced
Grass/dirt/
chips/gravel
Parking
Restroom
Seating
Small dog area
Trees
Water

Concerns

Dirt area can be a bit muddy, as can the grass

San Dimas Dog Park

301 Horsethief Canyon Road
(inside Horsethief Canyon Park)

Appears to be a nice park, but has some problems. Both the large and small dog sides have ample room to run. In the large dog area, however, there are spots where one's dog can be out of sight.

Green and lush, the shade areas are equipped with BBQ pits, which is risky for several reasons: hot coals, food in the park, people sitting, eating and paying little attention to their dogs.

There were rattlesnake warnings posted, as well as reminders that this is a wildlife area.

Local Veterinary Clinic

San Dimas Animal Hospital
San Dimas

909-599-1508

Amenities

Bulletin board
Clean-up
Disabled access
Double-gated
Entrances: 2
Fenced
Grass/dirt
Parking
Restroom
Seating
Shade structure
Small dog area
Trees
Water

Concerns

Flooding

Rattlesnake area

Areas on the slope where your dog is out of sight

BBQ pits

Knoll Hill Off-leash Dog Park

200 Knoll Drive

I have never seen so many trees in one dog park! I counted 76 young trees in the large dog area, and 24 in the small dog area.

The people in the park were pleasant but not terribly social when we were there, but I understand there is a regular crowd that gathers frequently. Would love to be there when the crowd is there!

A sign in the large dog area states "Large dogs only" but no one seems to pay attention to that.

Amenities

Bulletin board
Chips
Clean-up
Disabled access
Double-gated
Entrances: 2
Fenced
Restroom
Seating
Small dog area
Trees
Water

Concerns

Next to LA Port/ railroad tracks

Trees are quite young so shade is a bit scarce

These chips can be tough on dog feet

Local Veterinary Clinic

Rolling Hills Animal Hospital
Rancho Palos Verdes

310-831-1209

77

Sierra Madre Dog Park

611 East Sierra Madre Blvd.
(inside Sierra Madre Park)

This park is well secreted inside trees and bushes, and it takes a bit of a hunt. I almost left, and then spotted a gate and dog park entrance sign deep in the bushes next to what appears to be a junkyard.

These jungle-like overgrown park areas are a kid's hide-out dream but poor planning for a dog park that is surrounded by bushes and untrimmed greenery. The seating here is a bench and some old torn office chairs. Toys are strewn and chewed up. It appears to be well-used. A bit quirky. I don't like that your dogs are not visible at all times.

Special Hours: 6 am-10 pm

Local Veterinary Clinic

ASEC—Animal Emergency Center
Los Angeles

310-473-1561

Amenities

Clean-up
Double-gated
Entrances: 4
Fenced
Grass/dirt/gravel
Lights
Parking
Restroom
Seating
Small dog area
Trees
Water

Concerns

Fee: $5

Flooding

Permit required

Tricky to locate at back of the park

No disabled access

Laurel Canyon Dog Park

8260 Mulholand Drive

A huge park! Half of the large dog area was fenced off to replant grass seed. The small dog area is, indeed, small but shady and grassy for the little guys.

This park is clean and big enough to hold a good size group without getting too crowded. Many families in this park—kids in dog parks pose some significant risk.

A finger-paint artist set up his easel in the park and was offering to do paintings of your dog. Many of his works were on the fencing all the way around the park.

I really liked this park and will return!

Special Hours: 10 am-3 pm

Local Veterinary Clinic

Best Friends Animal Hospital
North Hollywood

818-766-2140
818-984-2698

Amenities

Bulletin board
Clean-up
Double-gated
Entrances: 3
Fenced
Grass/dirt
Parking
Restroom
Seating
Small dog area
Trees
Water

Concerns

Flooding

No disabled access

Rattlesnake area

Conejo Creek Dog Park

1350 Avenida de las Flores
(across street from Waverly Park)

Both sides of this park are very large! There is a lot of stretch out room, and this size is rarely seen in the small dog sections of parks.

Since there is no shade at this time (young trees) it can get hot on warm days, and very wet on rainy days. Come prepared.

People were very friendly throughout the park (I had to walk a ways to hit each end) and appeared proud of it. I was pleased with it, myself, and we will be back!

Amenities

Bulletin board
Clean-up
Disabled access
Double-gated
Entrances: 3
Fenced
Grass/dirt
Lights
Parking
Restroom
Seating
Shade structure
Small dog area
Trees
Water

Local Veterinary Clinic

Camino Animal Clinic, Inc.
Thousand Oaks

805-497-0969

Concerns

Trees are very young

Westminster Off-leash Dog Park

1234 Pacific Avenue

The big dog area is quite large and on a slope, while the small dog area is small—approximately 25' x 20'. The little guys got cheated!

The people at this park were very warm and welcoming, and the dogs got along very well.

There appears to be some problem with flooding at the bottom of the large dog area. A great hill for the dogs to run, and stretch full out.

But yes, what about the tiny tykes?

Special Hours: 6 am-10 pm

Amenities

Bulletin board
Clean-up
Double-gated
Entrances: 2
Fenced
Grass/chips
Parking
Seating
Shade structure
Small dog area
Trees
Water

Concerns

No disabled access

No restroom

Small dog area is very small

Local Veterinary Clinic

Calabasas Animal Clinic
Calabasas

818-880-0888

William S. Hart Park Dog Park

8341 De Longpre Avenue
(not the Hart Park in Newhall)

What a classy little park! What it lacks in size, it makes up for in charm. Very clean, well groomed and inviting.

This park is on a hillside inside a very green neighborhood. It is wonderfully peaceful, even with three 7 month old puppies racing and chasing, rolling in the chips, and being appropriately rowdy.

The people there were very welcoming. I was there at the time the founder of the park was there, which was a special treat. This is a favorite.

Amenities

Bulletin board
Chips
Clean-up
Disabled access
Double-gated
Entrances: 1
Fenced
Seating
Trees
Water

Concerns

No small dog area

No restrooms

Local Veterinary Clinic

Sunset Animal Hospital
Los Angeles

323-850-6952

Marin County

Canine Commons

Doherty near Magnolia
(inside Piper Park)

This is a favorite although Twyla did behave as though the chips were a bit tough on her little feet.

The people here are very nice and love to engage in conversation. Most of the dogs were under great control when we were there. Twyla fell head over heels for a Bernese Mountain Dog named Hamlet, and they followed each other around while enjoying the smells.

I have already visited this park several times—it is one of my faves.

Amenities

Chips
Clean-up
Double-gated
Entrances: 2
Fenced
Parking
Restroom
Seating
Small dog area
Trees
Water

Concerns

Trees very young—no shade

No disabled access

Shared staging area

Local Veterinary Clinic

Larkspur Landing
Veterinary Hospital
Larkspur Landing

415-461-6133

Dog Bone Meadow

Novato Blvd.,
north of San Marin Drive

This park is set up for the running dog and the walking person. There is a "track" of gravel that goes around the inside perimeter of the park, with agility equipment set up all along the path. The center of the park is green grass, and a great place to stretch four legs.

The people were quite warm, greeting newcomers eagerly. Very relaxed.

This definitely is one of my favorites. We have returned several times just to make sure!

Amenities

Agility equipment
Bulletin board
Clean-up
Disabled access
Double-gated
Entrances: 1
Fenced
Grass/dirt/gravel
Parking
Seating
Shade structure
Trees
Water

Concerns

No small dog area

No restrooms

Bushes make it hard to always see your dog

Can be windy

Local Veterinary Clinic

The Country Vet
Novato

415-897-8380

Marin Humane Society Dog Park

171 Bel Marin Keys Blvd.

Like the Marin Humane Society itself, this park was designed for the comfort of the animals and the people that visit. Quite green and shady, it made me want to sit on the dedicated benches and take a deep breath.

No one was there when I visited—restricted hours on the weekend are a shame! The hours closed to the public are so that the MHS staff and volunteers have access with the dogs.

A visit to the park should also mean a visit to the Humane Society! Go!

Special Hours: Sunrise-8:30 am & 4 pm—Sunset M-Th, Closed Fri. am.; Sunrise-8:30 am & 3 pm—Sunset Sat. & Sun. Can be reserved privately.

Local Veterinary Clinic

Veterinary Hospital of Ignacio
Novato

415-883-4626

Amenities

Clean-up
Disabled access
Double-dated
Entrances: 2
Fenced
Grass/chips/gravel & asphalt
Lights
Parking
Restroom
Seating
Shade structure
Small dog area
Trees
Water

Concerns

Fencing does not go all the way to the ground—sharp tips

Large dog area needs cloth fencing—very close to the street and could stimulate car chasing

Field of Dogs

Civic Center Drive
(next to the Fire Station)

There is good dog-community support here. At this writing there was some concern about the park closing and the city using the area to build, but no conclusion yet.

Provided are tennis balls galore, "chuck-its," and tennis rackets for those of us that throw poorly.

I did notice, however, that the gravel can be tough on feet, and have seen some older dogs standing still because their feet are uncomfortable. Otherwise, this is a nice park! We visit here regularly when in the area.

Amenities

Bulletin board
Clean-up
Disabled access
Double-gated
Entrances: 1
Fenced
Grass/dirt/gravel
Parking
Restroom
Seating
Shade structure
Small dog area
Trees
Water

Concerns

Foxtails

Small dog area is inside large area

Gravel rough on paws

Local Veterinary Clinic

Marin Pet Hospital
San Rafael

415-454-4414

Remington Dog Park

100 Ebbtide Avenue

This is a wonderful park. It is large, green and shady with great trees and landscape. It is on a long slope, and sometimes you can lose sight of your dog.

There are benches placed everywhere in the park, generally under the shade of the huge trees. A couch-potato heaven, but pay attention to your dog!

There is lots of user-policing of the park, assisting newcomers and keeping the park clean. We have been back a few times since our first visit. Good park!

Amenities

Bulletin board
Clean-up
Double-gated
Entrances: 1
Fenced
Grass/dirt/chips
Lights
Parking
Seating
Shade structure
Trees
Water

Concerns

No disabled access

No small dog area

May be escape areas along fence

No restroom

Local Veterinary Clinic

Sausalito Animal Hospital
Sausalito

415-332-2212

Napa County

Alston Park—Canine Commons

2099 Dry Creek Road

The wading pools and the hose are the popular areas when it's summer/fall. This park has lots of green bushes—caution, you can lose sight of your dog. It is warm and inviting. Very spacious in both the large and small dog areas.

There is open space nearby and some areas your dog can be leash-free, but other areas where dogs can be on leash only. Look for posted signs.

I liked this park a lot—the park community was warm and welcoming. We'll be back soon!

Amenities

Bulletin board
Clean-up
Double-gated
Entrances: 1
Fenced
Grass/dirt/chips
Parking
Restroom
Seating
Small dog area
Trees
Wading pools
Water

Concerns

No disabled access

You can easily lose sight of your dog

Parking can be tight

Local Veterinary Clinic

Napa Small Animal Hospital
Napa

707-257-8866

Orange County

Costa Mesa Bark Park

890 Arlington Drive
(inside TeWinkle Park)

I think this is a really nice park. Very friendly and social community in both large and small dog sides.

There are three bulletin boards with loads of community information. Chairs that have been donated by individuals abound in this park. The biggest concern was that there is a hilly area within the park, and you can lose sight of your dog while he's running and playing.

We will be back here!

Special Hours: Closed Tuesday

Amenities

Bulletin board
Clean-up
Disabled access
Double-gated
Entrances: 3
Fenced
Grass/dirt
Lights
Parking
Restroom
Seating
Small dog area
Trees
Water

Concerns

Closed on rainy days—flooding

Can't see your dog at all times

Local Veterinary Clinic

All Creatures Care
Cottage Veterinary Hospital
Costa Mesa

949-642-7151

Pooch Park

201 S. Basque Avenue

This park is next to the Hunt Branch Library. Unfortunately, the park was closed the day we stopped there—the rain was incredible, and the park sections were all flooded. All the gates were locked, so I assessed from outside the park.

There are three areas, two with trees, and one without. Given the signs and the boxes with literature, it is clear that this park is well supported by the users, as well as the city.

There is definitely good "karma" to this area, and I will return to let Twyla run in the future!

Amenities

Bulletin board
Clean-up
Disabled access
Double-gated
Entrances: 3
Fenced
Grass/dirt/chips
Lights
Parking
Restroom
Seating
Shade structure
Small dog area
Trees
Water

Local Veterinary Clinic

Airport Animal Hospital
Fullerton

714-879-4531

Concerns

Flooding

Restrooms appear to be in the library nearby

Best Friend Dog Park

Edwards Street and Talbert

This is a park with two very large areas. The fence in between the large dog and small dog areas are covered with green screens to cut down on fence running and interaction between the two areas.

One of the things I am seeing as a growing trend is water areas set on a cement block, and there is virtually no mess. Although one Golden Retriever repeatedly held water in his mouth and dumped it in the chips.

Nice welcoming atmosphere, and a good community. We will certainly be back to this park!

Amenities

Bulletin board
Clean-up
Disabled access
Double-gated
Entrances: 2
Fenced
Chips
Parking
Restroom
Seating
Shade structure
Small dog area
Trees
Water

Local Veterinary Clinic

Beach Blvd.
Veterinary Association
Huntington Beach

714-847-1291

Concerns

A lot of small children running in the park

Central Bark Dog Park

6405 Oak Canyon Road
(next to Irvine Animal Control)

Both sections of this park are very nice. Green, with shade around the outside perimeter. Large dog area, shaped like an "L," small dog area shaped like a box.

The community in this park is terrific, very cohesive and supportive of each other. They were all very welcoming on our arrival. Great monitoring of dogs and behavior.

This is one of my absolute favorites, and we would love to return here when we are in the area again!

Special Hours: Closed Wednesday

Amenities

Bulletin board
Clean-up
Disabled access
Double-gated
Entrances: 2
Fenced
Grass/dirt & gravel/asphalt
Lights
Parking
Restroom
Seating
Shade structure
Small dog area
Trees
Water

Local Veterinary Clinic

Irvine Pet Complex
Irvine

949-551-0304

Concerns

Flooding

Popular place for multi-dog professional dog walkers

Laguna Beach Bark Park

Laguna Canyon Road,
south of El Toro Road

The large dog area is huge! The drawback is that there is no shade inside the park, and trees are only outside the park, with the exception of a very young small tree in the small dog area. The water is only on the large dog side, so it must be bucketed in to the small dogs.

The community was close-knit and friendly. Quite an inviting atmosphere. The folks appeared quite responsible about watching their dogs and intervening at the first sign of disruption. We will be returning here. A favorite!

Special Hours: Closed Wednesday

Local Veterinary Clinic

South Coast Veterinary Hospital
Laguna Niguel

949-249-7777

Amenities

Bulletin board
Clean-up
Disabled access
Double-gated
Entrances: 2
Fenced
Grass/asphalt
Parking
Seating
Small dog area
Water

Concerns

No shade

No water in small dog area

No restroom

Muddy in wet weather

Laguna Niguel Dog Park

31461 Golden Lantern

This park is nicely landscaped, and the chips are small and fine, which appeared easy on Twyla's paws.

This park is very busy and open and has great running room. The bulletin board is next to a wall with plaques with the names of donors to the park.

The major flaw: the small dog area is set within the large dog area, so you must go through the large dogs to get to the safety of the small area. This area is also very small and without the amenities of the large dog area.

Amenities

Bulletin board
Clean-up
Entrances: 2
Fenced
Chips
Parking
Restroom
Seating
Shade structure
Small dog area
Trees
Water

Concerns

Small dog area is inside large dog area

Rattlesnake area

No disabled access

Local Veterinary Clinic

South Coast Veterinary Hospital
Laguna Niguel

949-249-7777

Laguna Woods Dog Park

Ridge Route & Peralta

This is a classic case of when the community of people make the park a good place to go. The people were wonderful, obviously a close-knit group that take care of each other and each other's pets when needed.

The park is under "construction" to lengthen it significantly, and it will also be narrowed. It is shady under a wonderful tree where there are benches, and it is a bit noisy with the zooming traffic. I liked this park. Good luck with the changes. I'll come back to see!

Special Hours: Small dogs: 8 am-1 pm; all size dogs together: 1-7 pm

Amenities

Bulletin board
Clean-up
Disabled access
Double-gated
Entrances: 1
Fenced
Grass/dirt
Parking
Seating
Trees
Water

Concerns

Busy street

No small dog area

No restroom

Local Veterinary Clinic

South Coast Veterinary Hospital
Laguna Niguel

949-249-7777

Loma Linda Dog Park

Beaumont St. & Mountain View
(inside Hulda Crooks Park)

The small dog area was moved recently up the hill and on the other side of the park. The large dog area is on a hillside and is the former small dog area which previously opened it up to a big joined section. It is grassy and woodsy, kind of a wild area, and you can lose sight of your dog at times.

The small dog area is up a different driveway, and is landscaped and green. There were several dogs playing when we arrived at each section, and people appeared to have good control.

The people were friendly and told me about other parks in the area. Thanks!

Amenities

Bulletin board
Clean-up
Double-gated
Entrances: 2
Fenced
Grass/dirt
Parking
Play structures
Restroom
Seating
Small dog area
Trees
Water

Local Veterinary Clinic

Moreno Valley Animal Hospital
Moreno Valley

951-242-2111

Concerns

Large and small dog areas are in different locations

No disabled access

Orange Dog Park

190 S. Yorba Street
(inside Yorba Park)

Even though this park is directly next to a freeway, and is noisy, it still has ambience. The large dog area is the size of the athletic field, while the small dog area is significantly more compact. The small area is shady and green while there is limited shade in the large dog area.

The community here is very involved in this park, with an organization called Orange Dog Park Association.

There were only a few people at the park when we visited, but I'm told it fills up at the usual times: evenings and weekends. We will return to this one!

Special Hours: Closed Wednesday

Local Veterinary Clinic

Orange-Olive Veterinary Hospital
Orange

714-998-1510

Amenities

Bulletin board
Clean-up
Disabled access
Double-gated
Entrances: 2
Fenced
Grass/dirt/gravel
Parking
Restroom
Seating
Small dog area
Trees
Water

Concerns

Flooding

Next to a freeway

Baron von Willard Memorial Dog Park

301 Avenida La Pata

This park is dedicated to a German Shepherd—the first San Clemente Police K-9, who died in the line of duty.

The view of the valley from this park is astounding. It is worth the drive just to get the view, but the park is very nice as well. It is clearly cared about, well-groomed and clean. The gravel is fairly large, however, and can be hard on running paws as evidenced by Twyla's sore feet after a good romp here.

It was a quiet Saturday when we visited, people were very sweet and proud of their park. We will return here.

Amenities

Bulletin board
Clean-up
Double-gated
Entrances: 1
Fenced
Grass/gravel
Parking
Seating
Shade structure
Small dog area
Water

Concerns

No disabled access

No restroom

No trees

Large sized gravel

Local Veterinary Clinic

Pacific Coast Veterinarians
San Clemente

949-429-1555

Orange County—Seal Beach

Arbor Dog Park

4665 Lampson Avenue
(between Heather and Rose)

Located behind the large West Ed building, it can be tricky to find.

This park was alive and kickin' on our visit. Big dogs galloping through the large area. Open and inviting, trees are scattered here and there.

There are 3 bulletin boards—a little something for everyone. There is no small dog area, and I saw some little guys hanging out in laps at the seating areas with their people for security while the big guys played.

We enjoyed the camaraderie at this park, and will return!

Amenities

Bulletin board
Clean-up
Double-gated
Entrances: 2
Fenced
Grass/dirt
Parking
Restroom
Trees
Water

Concerns

No disabled access

No small dog area

Local Veterinary Clinic

Garden Grove Dog
and Cat Hospital
Long Beach

562-490-9432

Placer County

Ashley Memorial Dog Park

Auburn Ravine Road
(inside Ashford Park)

When we entered this lovely area, the park was only 4 weeks old, and finishing touches were in progress. Planned were a waterfall/fountain feature at one end.

This used to be a soccer field and is quite open. Dogs can stretch out and tire themselves out.

Apparently the park is well-used; it is the only one for many miles. The people were very sweet and hospitable and enjoyed talking about their park.

I liked it, and I'll be back!

Amenities

Clean-up
Disabled access
Double-gated
Entrances: 1
Fenced
Grass/chips
and gravel
Parking
Restroom
Seating
Shade structure
Small dog area
Trees
Wading pools
Water

Local Veterinary Clinic

Evening Pet Clinic
Auburn

530-888-7387

Concerns

Flooding

Rattlesnake area

Bear Dog Park

1575 Pleasant Grove Blvd.

This park is sponsored by the local animal control, as are many new parks throughout the state. Hurray for them! I love to see them involved.

There is no agility equipment in the small dog area, so most people use the large dog area.

There are two small asphalt fenced areas with hoses for dog showers. Each little area is privately fenced.

Great people, very warm. Like home, only dustier...

Special Hours: Closed Tuesday until 10 am

Amenities

Agility equipment
Bulletin board
Clean-up
Disabled access
Double-gated
Entrances: 1
Fenced
Grass/dirt/gravel
Lights
Parking
Restroom
Seating
Small dog area
Trees
Water

Local Veterinary Clinic

Arbor View Veterinary Clinic
Roseville

916-789-2211

Concerns

Trees are young, so shade is slim— can be hot

Marco Dog Park

1800 Sierra Gardens Drive

Chairs everywhere indicate this park is well-used. Lots of folks were there when we were there.

The entrance has a partially fenced asphalt walkway from the street down to the ravine—prevents gate-rushing and allows dog to see the area before entering.

Good people and great feel to this park! The community is very strong in this very large park.

Can we visit this every day?

Special Hours: Closed Wed.

Amenities

Bulletin board
Clean-up
Disabled access
Double-gated
Entrances: 1
Fenced
Grass/dirt
Restroom
Seating
Shade structure
Trees
Wading pools
Water

Concerns

Busy street

In a ravine behind shopping center

Flooding

No small dog area

Local Veterinary Clinic

Arbor View Veterinary Clinic
Roseville

916-789-2211

William Hughes Park Dog Park

Parkside Drive at Eskaton Loop

This was challenging to find due to construction of new homes in the area. The dog park is on the south side of the park near the basketball courts and the soccer field.

Three sections make up this park—large dog, small dog, and a third that can be used for shy or aggressive dogs, or for obedience training. Each park can be opened to the other to make one large space. Small dog area has no amenities.

Nice people and community.

Special Hours: Closed Thursday until 10 am

Local Veterinary Clinic

Arbor View Veterinary Clinic
Roseville

916-789-2211

Amenities

Disabled access
Double-gated
Entrances: 2
Fenced
Grass/dirt
Hose
Lights
Parking
Restroom
Seating
Small dog area
Trees
Water

Concerns

No clean up

No water in the small dog area

No seating in small dog area

Riverside County

Butterfield Dog Park

1886 Butterfield Drive
(inside Butterfield Stage Trail Park)

Butterfield Park is serious about cleaning up after your dog—there are cement trash receptacles and poop bags available every few feet.

Lots of shade. This park is quite relaxing. Open areas are great for running. Unfortunately, when we visited there were no small dogs — Twyla walked in, stood there, then looked at me as if to say "Where is everybody?" I can tell the area is well used as indicated by the paw and skid marks in the dirt.

The community of people made us feel right at home. We'll be back!

Amenities

Bulletin board
Clean-up
Disabled access
Double-gated
Entrances: 2
Fenced
Grass/dirt
Lights
Parking
Restroom
Seating
Small dog area
Trees
Water

Local Veterinary Clinic

Animal Care Wellness Center
San Bernadino

909-883-6464

Concerns

Busy street

Water is outside the fenced areas

Harada Heritage Dog Park

13100 65th Street

Inside a large new housing development, this small park is a handsome
addition to the neighborhood. It has a
decent stretch-out area in both the large
and small dog sections.

Nothing fancy about this place but it is
young and new. It is extremely clean
and kept up nicely. The cement
walkways are nice if someone has
challenged mobility.

The weather was rough when we
visited, so no other users, but it appears
to get a lot of use. I liked this park.

Special Hours: Closed Wednesday
am

Amenities

Bulletin board
Clean-up
Disabled access
Double-gated
Entrances: 2
Fenced
Grass/asphalt
Lights
Parking
Seating
Small dog area
Trees
Water

Local Veterinary Clinic

Animal Care Wellness Center
San Bernadino

909-883-6464

Concerns

No shade—trees
are quite young

No restroom

Civic Center Dog Park

43900 San Pablo Avenue &
Fred Waring Drive

I have not been to a park (other than this one) that had cooling mist come out of the shade structure in the small dog area at the push of a button on the structure. Wow. Great way to beat the heat. I felt so pampered!

This is one of my absolute favorites. Lush and green, shady trees, wonderful people, and many of the dogs were rescue dogs. There is lots of running room in each section—large and small. The fencing is beautiful black rod iron, and the park is clean and well-groomed.

I might move here just for the dog park.

Amenities

Clean-up
Disabled access
Double-gated
Entrances: 2
Fenced
Grass/gravel
Lights
Parking
Restroom
Seating
Shade structure
with misters
Small dog area
Trees
Water

Local Veterinary Clinic

Animal Hospital of Desert
Palm Desert

760-568-5151

Concerns

Shared staging

Freedom Dog Park

77-400 Country Club Drive

This postage stamp sized fenced dog park is located inside a beautifully landscaped brand new city park with all the bells and whistles.

It is nicely landscaped, but has absolutely no running room. One guy threw a ball lightly for his dog and it hit the fence almost before it left his hand.

On hot days, this park is close to unbearable. The shade structure seemed to attract the heat.

We stayed a very short time.

Amenities

Bulletin board
Clean-up
Disabled access
Double-gated
Entrances: 2
Fenced
Grass
Lights
Parking
Restroom
Seating
Shade structure
Small dog area
Trees
Water

Local Veterinary Clinic

Animal Hospital of Desert
Palm Desert

760-568-5151

Concerns

Shared staging

Very small

No water in small dog area

Joe Mann Park Dog Park

Avenue of the States &
California Avenue

This park is next to the Country Club. It is well-groomed and clean, and the grass is very green for this time of year.

It is quite a small park, and the small dog area is a postage stamp that looks like an after-thought.

Twyla ran and ran with a Basenji named Chase and a young Pit Bull named Bella. The people in this park were wonderful and welcoming.

We will surely be back!

Special Hours: Closed Tuesday am

Amenities

Clean-up
Disabled access
Double-gated
Entrances: 2
Fenced
Grass/gravel
Parking
Restroom
Seating
Shade structure
Small dog area
Trees
Water

Concerns

Shared staging

Lots of flying gnats, but it was late summer when we visited

Local Veterinary Clinic

Animal Hospital of Desert
Palm Desert

760-568-5151

Palm Springs Dog Park

222 Civic Drive North

This is one of the absolute best parks we visited. The fencing is beautiful, the people are extremely welcoming and the park is very clean! The small dog area is apparently fairly new.

I stayed for a couple of hours. The park was our last visit that day, the evening was calm and balmy, and I couldn't tear myself away from the people.

Apparently, City Hall (directly across the street) is very supportive of this park. How I wish they all were! I also wish I lived closer to this park, but we will be back!

Special Hours: Dawn-10 pm

Local Veterinary Clinic

Moreno Valley Animal Hospital
Moreno Valley

951-242-2111

Amenities

Bulletin board
Clean-up
Disabled access
Double-gated
Entrances: 3
Fenced
Grass/asphalt
Lights
Parking
Seating
Shade structure
Small dog area
Trees
Water

Concerns

3 entrances, so owners need to be watchful with an escape artist when people are coming and going

No restroom

Pat Merritt Dog Park

Limonite Frontage Road &
Emery Street

Wonderful park—very green and open, and kept incredibly clean.

The layout is nice—the two areas separated by a courtyard, that has trees and bushes. One drawback is that the large dog area has a small hill that makes it difficult to see your dog at all times. The growing mushrooms can be a problem for dogs that like to eat everything in their path.

The folks we met were inviting, and we will definitely return to play again.

Amenities

Bulletin board
Clean-up
Double-gated
Entrances: 4
Fenced
Grass
Lights
Parking
Seating
Shade structure
Small dog area
Trees
Water

Concerns

No restroom

No disabled access

Can lose sight of your dog

Mushrooms growing in park

Local Veterinary Clinic

Riverside Animal Hospital, Inc.
Riverside

951-683-4200

Riverwalk Dog Park

Pierce Street & Collett Avenue

We were unable to visit this park, but got the scoop on most amenities and the community.

Apparently this park can get pretty hot on warm days. It is very nicely land-scaped, but the trees are young and need some time to provide shade. It does have a large and small dog area, with the parking lot set in between the two—I like that sort of separation because shy small dogs aren't overwhelmed by the big guys on the other side of the fence, also cutting down on fence-running.

People spoke positively about this dog area, and I look forward to visiting here with Twyla on our return.

Amenities

Clean-up
Double-gated
Entrances: 2
Fenced
Parking
Seating
Small dog area
Trees (young)
Water

Concerns

Disabled access unknown

Can get warm

Local Veterinary Clinic

Riverside Animal Hospital, Inc.
Riverside

951-683-4200

Temecula Dog Exercise Area

Redhawk Parkway
(between Paseo Parallon &
Via Rio Temecula)

I was told this is the best fenced dog park in the area. I was then told it is the only fenced dog park in the area.

The large and small dog areas are next to each other so there was some fence-running with a pack of small dogs, Twyla trying to join the mix as usual.

Nice people, and most folks owned rescued dogs—a definite plus. The community appears strong and connected. Twyla ran until she collapsed in the grass. We'll be back!

Special Hours: Closed Friday am

Local Veterinary Clinic

Butterfield Animal Hospital
Temecula

951-303-8260

Amenities

Bulletin board
Clean-up
Double-gated
Entrances: 2
Fenced
Grass/dirt
Parking
Restroom
Seating
Small dog area
Trees

Concerns

No water

No disabled access

Shared staging

Sacramento County

Carmichael Park Canine Corral

5750 Grant Avenue

This park is located by the softball diamond, behind the postal distribution station, so it can be a bit noisy.

Good social network here, welcoming atmosphere. Everyone seemed to have great control of their dogs as they played.

The wading pools were especially popular when we visited due to the heat.

The large dog side had a very big running area. I liked this park very much. We'll be back.

Amenities

Clean-up
Disabled access
Double-gated
Entrances: 2
Fenced
Grass/dirt
Lights
Parking
Restroom
Seating
Small dog area
Trees
Wading pools
Water

Local Veterinary Clinic

Hazel Ridge Veterinary Clinic
Fair Oaks

916-965-8200

Concerns

Flooding—can be very muddy

Lots of fence-running between big and small dog parks

C-Bar-C Park

8275 Oak Avenue

This is the first park that we stayed in for a two-hour stretch. The atmosphere was relaxed and social, and I made some friends there that I am still in touch with.

This is the favorite dog park for many miles around. It is certainly one of the top that we've seen.

Due to the warm weather, the wading pools in both sides were well-used, and full of splashing Labs and Beagles.

Don't miss this park! We'll be back.

Special Hours: Closed Thursday am

Local Veterinary Clinic

Hazel Ridge Veterinary Clinic
Fair Oaks

916-965-8200

Amenities

Bulletin board
Clean-up
Double-gated
Entrances: 2
Fenced
Grass/dirt
Parking
Restroom
Seating
Small dog area
Trees
Wading pools
Water

Concerns

No disabled access

Trees are still young

Elk Grove Dog Park

9950 Elk Grove Florin Road
(inside Elk Grove Regional Park)

This is a very nice dog park within a very nice park. Both are very well groomed and green.

The social scene is quite active, and the park was very busy when we visited. We were welcomed warmly and people were eager to share stories about their dogs with me.

It can get a bit muddy at the water fountain, and several dogs were a murky shade of brown. Twyla tip-toed to the water bowl and got out of there as fast as possible.

I really liked this park.

Amenities

Agility equipment
Bulletin board
Clean-up
Double-gated
Entrances: 1
Fenced
Grass
Parking
Restroom
Seating
Trees
Water

Concerns

Quite windy

Disabled access questionable

No small dog area

Can be muddy

Local Veterinary Clinic

Bradshaw Veterinary Clinic
Elk Grove

916-685-2494

Laguna Dog Park

Big Horn Blvd. &
Monterey Oaks Drive

While this is a nice, well-groomed and attractive park, it is too small for a large dog to get in a good run. It is small enough to have a conversation on the other side of the park without shouting. I question the safety of this park for large and small dogs to congregate together. It is easily filled beyond capacity.

The people we met were very friendly and welcoming. A decent park to take Twyla for a quick walk and sniff, when it's not busy.

Amenities

Clean-up
Disabled access
Double-gated
Entrances: 1
Fenced
Grass
Parking
Seating
Shade structure
Trees
Water

Concerns

No restroom

No small dog area

Small run area

Local Veterinary Clinic

Bradshaw Veterinary Clinic
Elk Grove

916-685-2494

Phoenix Dog Park

9050 Sunset Avenue

Very nice park. Great social atmosphere and friendly people.

This park is well-groomed and clean, with loads of running stretch-out room in both areas. There is also a third fenced area for shy or dog-aggressive dogs to play without threatening or being threatened.

The water fountain areas are on cement "pads" and therefore have no mud! How soon can we go back?

Amenities

Bulletin board
Clean-up
Double-gated
Entrances: 2
Fenced
Grass/asphalt
Parking
Restroom
Seating
Shade structure
Small dog area
Trees
Water

Local Veterinary Clinic

Bradshaw Veterinary Clinic
Elk Grove

916-685-2494

Concerns

Trees are outside the park

No disabled access

Shared staging

FIDO Field

1775 Creekside Drive
(in Cummings Family Park)

This park was only one month old
when we visited. Many locals are
relieved to have some place close by to
exercise their dogs. It's a nice park
area and I enjoyed the visit.

Unfortunately, the majority of users
when we were there were new to the
dog park scene and lacked some sense
of control and interpreting their dog's
body language. But with time, they
appeared to relax, and were talked to
and educated by more seasoned dog
park users.

We will go back to see how the park
matures.

Amenities

Clean-up
Disabled access
Double-gated
Entrances: 1
Fenced
Grass/dirt/chips
Lights
Parking
Restroom
Seating
Shade structure
Small dog area
Trees
Water

Local Veterinary Clinic

Folsom Veterinary Hospital
Folsom

916-985-4700
800-648-9272

Concerns

Flooding

Rattlesnake area

Trees are young -
no shade

Tanzanite Dog Park

Tanzanite Drive near
Innovator Drive

This park has good potential when the young trees grow a bit. It is a long park, that runs along the side of a green lush area surrounding a large pond. The dog park has gate-access to the pond, but the pond itself is not fenced.

A popular park—people apparently travel from all over the area to visit here.

In a newly built housing development, so everything is brand new and shiny. We'll be back!

Amenities

Clean-up
Disabled access
Double-gated
Entrances: 1
Fenced
Grass/dirt
Parking
Restroom
Seating
Trees
Water

Concerns

Flooding

No small dog area

Pond has no fence

Near skateboard and bike park

Trees not planted near cemented benches

Local Veterinary Clinic

Atlantic Street
Veterinary Hospital &
Pet Emergency Center
Roseville

916-783-4655

Regency Dog Park

Honor Parkway & Bridgecross
(next to Regency Community Park)

This park was tricky to find because though it shares the name, it is not inside the Regency Park. It can be quite hot in the summer as the trees are very young and provided little shade.

We noticed many young dog owners—teens—who were all very proud of their dogs but needed some coaching on dog park etiquette and basic dog behavior in parks.

This park is in the middle of new housing developments, has a ways to go to mature.

I'll return to watch its progress!

Amenities

Disabled access
Double-gated
Entrances: 2
Fenced
Grass/chips
and gravel
Lights
Parking
Seating
Small dog area
Trash cans
Trees
Water

Concerns

No restroom

No poop bags

Trees very young
so not much shade

Local Veterinary Clinic

Atlantic Street
Veterinary Hospital &
Pet Emergency Center
Roseville

916-783-4655

Westside Dog Park

West 2nd Street near M Street
(inside Westside Park)

This park was barren, full of stickers and prickly ground cover, not maintained at all, and the trees were too young for any shade whatsoever.

Backed up against a horse training ring, there were two large black dogs in the horse area that ran the fence, barking and growling. No one else was at the park, can you figure why?

I won't be back here.

Amenities

Dirt
Entrances: 1
Parking
Seating
Trees
Water

Concerns

Flooding

Foxtails/stickers

Young trees

No small dog area

No Clean-up

No restroom

Shoddy fencing

No disabled access

Local Veterinary Clinic

Atlantic Street
Veterinary Hospital &
Pet Emergency Center
Roseville

916-783-4655

Bannon Creek Dog Park

Bannon Creek Drive & Azevedo Drive

This park is very small and cozy. Lots of trees and tons of seating areas.

Unfortunately this park is prone to flooding. When we visited it had been over 2 weeks since it had rained and there were still significant areas of mud.

We were alone at this park—no takers on a warm sunny weekend day.

Without the mud, this little park has lots of charm. Great for a planned small dog gathering.

Special Hours: 5 am-10 pm

Local Veterinary Clinic

Del Paso Veterinary Clinic
Sacramento

916-925-2107

Amenities

Clean-up
Disabled access
Double-gated
Entrances: 1
Fenced
Grass/asphalt
Seating
Trees
Water

Concerns

Flooding

No small dog area

No restroom

Challenging to find

Granite Dog Park

Power Inn Road & Ramona Avenue
(inside Granite Park)

This park is located behind the Courthouse, near a skateboard park.

Lots of family groups, a lot of dogs at the park when we visited. However, there was no socializing between groups or individuals, everyone seemed isolated and unapproachable. This atmosphere made me feel unwelcome, and while this may not be the norm at this park, it was a little disconcerting.

The park grounds are nice, although can be hot.

Special Hours: 5 am-10 pm

Local Veterinary Clinic

Del Paso Veterinary Clinic
Sacramento

916-925-2107

Amenities

Clean-up
Disabled access
Double-gated
Entrances: 4
Fenced
Grass/dirt/gravel
Parking
Restroom
Seating
Shade structure
Trees
Wading pools
Water

Concerns

No small dog area

Can be very hot, not a lot of shade

People seemed isolated and not engaged

Can be windy

Howe About Dogs

Cottage Way near Howe Avenue

Located between the tennis courts and the baseball field, you must drive to the back of the parking lot.

This park is relatively small, but has a great set-up for running in the open area. A lot of shade trees keep this area cool on hot days.

The dog owners were all very friendly, and we arrived to join a bevy of pit bull puppies, gathered to socialize. (Bumbling puppies are Twyla's favorite.)

We'll be back to this one.

Amenities

Clean-up
Disabled access
Double-gated
Entrances: 1
Fenced
Grass
Parking
Seating
Trees
Water

Concerns

Busy street—be sure to leash your dog coming and going

No small dog area

No restroom

Local Veterinary Clinic

Del Paso Veterinary Clinic
Sacramento

916-925-2107

Partner Park

5699 South Land Park Drive
(behind Belle Coolidge
Community Center)

This park is extremely green and lush. Very, very clean and well-cared for by the city. One of my concerns is not being able to see my dog at all times.

A relatively large park, the dogs seemed to have fun running up and down the hills, racing and chasing. We played with Joey, a three-legged Pit bull pup, and Ruckus, a Lab/Pointer mix. Twyla seemed to have a great time, but tired out quickly in the heat.

The people in the park were extremely jovial and friendly, and I look forward to going back!

Special Hours: Closed Friday am

Local Veterinary Clinic

Del Paso Veterinary Clinic
Sacramento

916-925-2107

Amenities

Clean-up
Disabled access
Double-gated
Entrances: 1
Fenced
Grass/dirt
Lights
Parking
Restroom
Seating
Trees
Water

Concerns

Busy street

No small dog area

Large trunked trees and hilly areas make it hard to see your dog from many parts of the park

Sam Combs Dog Park

205 Stone Blvd.
(inside Sam Combs Park)

_____

Wow! Lots of big oak trees filling the park with shade — it's wonderful on crunchy leaves, but they can be messy and slippery in the rain.

There are fire hydrants for the boy dogs, and a few females, as well as wading pools and hoses on each side. It can be muddy at the water fountains.

This one is flat, green and shady, and a paradise for those just watching the dogs romp. This was definitely one of my favorites!

Amenities

Clean-up
Disabled access
Double-gated
Entrances: 2
Fenced
Grass/dirt
Parking
Seating
Small dog area
Trees
Wading pools
Water

Concerns

Busy street— on leash to and from the park

Flooding

Wet fallen leaves can be slippery

No restroom

Local Veterinary Clinic

El Camino Veterinary
Hospital, Inc.
Sacramento

916-488-6878

San Bernadino County

Highland Dog Park

Greenspot Road
(south of 5th Street)

This is a really nice park, very clean, well-groomed and landscaped. But no small dog area in such a big dog park!

The community appears to be quite cohesive for the most part. We were warmly welcomed and included in the social group.

There were several dogs in the park that were running and chasing full out. A little risky with the mix of large and small dogs.

Nice people in a pretty park.

Amenities

Bulletin board
Clean-up
Disabled access
Double-gated
Entrances: 1
Fenced
Grass
Parking
Restroom
Seating
Shade structure
Water

Concerns

No trees, just two gazebo areas

No small dog area

Rattlesnake area

Local Veterinary Clinic

Highland Village Pet Hospital
Highland

909-864-7387

Rancho Cucamonga Dog Park

East Avenue near Banyan
(inside Etiwanda Creek Park)

This is a nice park, full of green and trees. The large dog area provides great running space, and lots of shade.

The small dog area is very small, and when we were there it was also quite dirty with pup-poop. May have just been the day. There is shared staging area from the street entrance.

Most of the people were very welcoming. There was good responsibility for their dogs and behavior.

Amenities

Bulletin board
Clean-up
Disabled access
Double-gated
Entrances: 2
Fenced
Grass/dirt/gravel
Parking
Restroom
Seating
Small dog area
Trees
Water

Concerns

Can be muddy in the rain

Local Veterinary Clinic

Rancho Regional Veterinary
Rancho Cucamonga

909-941-0841

Wildwood Park Dog Park

4999 N. Waterman Avenue &
40th Street

The entry area here is a bit confusing—lots of gates to lots of areas. There are three areas—two big areas and one very small area. The smallest area has nothing more than water and one bench, but the larger areas are fully equipped.

Lots of green grass and big shady trees, inside both of the larger areas side by side. If you look up to the outside of the park, there are high desert hills filled with desert plants.

The people we met were great, friendly and funny and welcoming. If we lived nearby, we would be here often!

Amenities

Bulletin board
Clean-up
Double-gated
Entrances: 3
Fenced
Grass/dirt
Lights
Parking
Restroom
Seating
Small dog area
Trees
Water

Concerns

No water in smallest area

Rattlesnake area

Confined staging area

No disabled access

Local Veterinary Clinic

Animal Care Wellness Center
San Bernadino

909-883-6464

Baldy View Dog Park

11th Street (between
Mountain Avenue & San Antonio)

_____

Beautifully laid out! Lush, green and
shady. Can get muddy in the rain. The
small dog area is not as pretty as the
large, and it has a gate that you can
open into the large dog area.

The community here is very nice and
welcoming. Twyla demonstrated that
the perimeter of the park had the best
smells, and she tip-toed through the
wet grass. She did however, hook up
with a young Irish Setter to get some
good wags in.

I would use this park daily if I could!

Amenities

Bulletin board
Clean-up
Double-gated
Entrances: 2
Fenced
Grass/dirt
Parking
Restroom
Seating
Small dog area
Trees
Water

Concerns

Flooding

Shared staging

No disabled access

Fencing/hedge is
only 3 feet high

Local Veterinary Clinic

Foothill Animal Hospital
Upland

909-985-1988

San Diego County

Carlsbad Dog Park

Carlsbad Village Drive
(between El Camino & Concord)

This a nice little park with some very nice folks. When we visited, it was raining, and there were a few brave souls that arrived with their dogs who barely seemed to notice the wet.

The chips spread on the ground in this park are small and seemed easy on dog feet, and the park didn't have a speck of mud in the rain!

There is a large, long staging area at the entrance, a nice set up for dogs to see the dogs throughout the park prior to entry. I liked this park a lot.

Amenities

Clean-up
Double-gated
Entrances: 1
Fenced
Chips
Parking
Restroom
Seating
Trees
Water

Concerns

No small dog area

No disabled access

No water

Local Veterinary Clinic

Drake Center for Veterinary Care
Encinitas

760-753-9393

Montevalle Dog Park

840 Duncan Ranch Road

Wonderful park! One of my faves.

Entry area is gravel, with grass that goes up an easy rise. Small dog area is half the size of the large dog area.

While we were at the park, there was a bevy of Welsh Corgis that ran the park with Twyla joining in, leaping and jumping and running.

Very social group, very welcoming. All were responsible—cleaning up and controlling their dogs.

Great community. Really nice park.

Amenities

Clean-up
Disabled access
Double-gated
Entrances: 2
Fenced
Grass/Gravels
Parking
Restroom
Seating
Small dog area
Trees
Water

Concerns

Can be hot—attendees really want the trees to hurry up and grow

Small dogs do a lot of fence-running with the dogs in the large area

Local Veterinary Clinic

South Bay Veterinary Hospital
Chula Vista

619-422-6186

Veteran's Park Dog Area

785 East Palomar Street
(inside Veteran's Park)

This little park is clearly well-used, given the number of beat-up tennis balls scattered around, and the skid marks in the gravel surface. However, it is quite small to accommodate many dogs at one time.

There are young trees, but not placed anywhere near the benches provided. The dog area is within a large beautifully landscaped park. The large park as well as the dog area are very clean!

Finding the dog area is challenging—it is up the hill behind the softball field.

Amenities

Clean-up
Double-gated
Entrances: 1
Fenced
Gravel
Restroom
Seating
Street parking
Trees
Water

Concerns

No disabled access

No small dog area

Benches are metal with holes that small paws could get caught in

Local Veterinary Clinic

South Bay Veterinary Hospital
Chula Vista

619-422-6186

Well's Park Dog Park

1153 E. Madison Avenue

_____

This park has wonderful shade trees and is nice and cool on hot days. Very pretty park. Located behind the children's play area. Very clean park.

The community appears to be quite friendly, and know each other well.

The regulars were quite inviting and warm upon our arrival. Demonstrated a lot of responsibility for their dog's behavior and clean-up.

I was told by park regulars that this area may not be safe after dusk, but no problems during the day.

Special Hours: 7 am-9 pm

Amenities

Clean-up
Disabled access
Double-gated
Entrances: 1
Fenced
Grass/gravel
Parking
Restroom
Seating
Shade structure
Small dog area
Trees
Water

Concerns

Possibly not safe area at night

Gravel cover is very harsh on dog feet—sharp

Local Veterinary Clinic

Care and Comfort
Veterinary Hospital
El Cajon

619-590-6160

Rancho Coastal Humane Dog Park

389 Requeza Street

One of my top parks! I loved this place, not to mention the fact that I think this is one of the best Humane Societies I have visited. It's not fancy, but the dogs and cats have thick bedding and outside heating.

This park is beautifully landscaped, with hills and turns and lots of great play areas. Some of the bushes make it difficult to always see your dog.

Great people, in and out of the park, the shelter staff is terrific. We will be back to this "puppy."

Special Hours: 11 am- 5 pm

Amenities

Bulletin board
Clean-up
Disabled access
Double-gated
Entrances: 2
Fenced
Grass/dirt
Parking
Restroom
Seating
Shade structure
Small dog area
Trees
Water

Local Veterinary Clinic

Drake Center for Veterinary Care
Encinitas

760-753-9393

Concerns

Closed in rain

Disabled access only into large dog area, none to small dog area

Mayflower Dog Park

Valley Parkway and Beven Street

There are three dog areas in this park, and a commercial agility area across the parking lot, used for classes only.

The folks we met were very nice. Buddy (a young Papillion) and Zues (a mature Great Dane mix) played wonderfully with Twyla.

The three areas are quite spacious, although the sections are not marked for dog size, so it appears to change off frequently. But we will return, as this was a lovely experience.

Special Hours: Dawn-9 pm

Local Veterinary Clinic

Creekside Veterinary Service
Escondido

760-728-2319

Amenities

Bulletin board
Clean-up
Disabled access
Entrances: 2
Fenced
Grass/dirt/asphalt
Lights
Parking
Restroom
Seating
Small dog area
Trees
Water

Concerns

Told by HS staff nearby that sometimes dogs are not well controlled, however I did not witness that

Small and large dog areas are interchangeable

Harry Griffen Park Dog Park

9550 Milden Street

This park has three areas: large, small and one for less social dogs. The bulletin board area is very full and clearly the park goers are quite active in the dog community. Cement benches throughout the park have dedications etched into them. Decorative dog-bone plaques surround the fence on the inside of the park. The park is clearly supported by local businesses with banners throughout the park.

Nice large areas although some people seemed quite isolated inside the park.

Amenities

Bulletin board
Clean-up
Dirt/gravel
Double-gated
Entrances: 1
Fenced
Parking
Restroom
Seating
Shade structure
Small dog area
Trees
Water

Concerns

One double-gated staging area

No disabled access

Can be very dusty

Challenging to find

Local Veterinary Clinic

Eastridge Veterinary Clinic
La Mesa

619-465-5291

NCHS Off-leash Dog Park

2905 San Luis Rey Road
(North County Humane Society)

This hilly park is great for running up and down the area, leaping and playing. There were dogs playing with tennis balls all by themselves—running to the top of the hill and rolling the ball down the slope to chase.

The North County Humane Society owns this park and is right next door. I had some concerns that when you are at the top or bottom of the hill in the large dog area, your dog is easily out of site at the opposite end.

The community was very welcoming, and my tour of the accompanying shelter was uplifting—great staff and volunteers at this facility.

Special Hours: Closed Wed. & in rain

Local Veterinary Clinic

Rancho Del Oro
Veterinary Hospital
Oceanside

760-945-0606

Amenities

Bulletin board
Clean-up
Disabled access
Double-gated
Entrances: 1
Fenced
Grass/dirt
Seating
Shade structure
Small dog area
Trees
Water

Concerns

Can be muddy

Can't always see your large dog due to the hilly landscape in the large dog area

No restroom

Poway Dog Park

13094 Bowron Road

This park actually has three fenced areas: large dog, small dog and a neutral area for shy or aggressive dogs. Two of these areas were closed at the time we visited for construction and improvements.

Lots of large trees, provided great shade. The tables are located under the trees—nice seating area. There are several areas to enter or exit the park, which can be risky for escaping dogs.

The people were quite friendly and very social. The big dogs had a great time running in the large open area.

Special Hours: Dawn-9:30 pm

Local Veterinary Clinic

Poway Animal Hospital
Poway

858-748-3326

Amenities

Clean-up
Dirt/grass
Disabled access
Double-gated
Entrances: 4
Fenced
Lights
Parking
Restroom
Seating
Shade structure
Small dog area
Telephone
Trees
Water

Concerns

All but the large dog area was under construction at the time we visited

Capeheart Park Dog Park

Soledad Mountain Road &
Feldspar Street

I enjoyed this park. The large dog and the small dog areas are completely separated by the parking lot so there is no cross-over contact. That is very nice for shy or cautious small dogs that are afraid of big dogs. There are bulletin boards at each park area.

The community was very welcoming and directed us to other parks in the area.

The small dog area has a table and umbrella to provide shade. We both enjoyed being here. I'll go back.

Special Hours: Open 24 hours

Local Veterinary Clinic

Turquoise Animal Hospital
San Diego

858-488-0658

Amenities

Bulletin boards
Clean-up
Disabled access
Double-gated
Entrances: 2
Fenced
Grass/dirt
Parking
Restroom
Seating
Small dog area
Water

Concerns

Busy street

Rattlesnake area

No shade in the large dog area—can be a hot park

Doyle Community Park Dog Park

Cargill Avenue,
south of Nobel Drive

This is a nice park with a good community of people that appeared very knowledgeable about the rules and history of their park.

The large dog area tends to have flooding and mud issues, so the water has been removed from that area and is only available in the small dog area. Containers are filled there and brought in to the large dog area.

It is a well-used park, and was chock full of large dogs when we visited, but a bit low (no pun) on small dogs, but Twyla did find a few buddies to romp with her.

Special Hours: 24 hours, but closed Tuesday and Thursday Noon-2 pm

Amenities

Bulletin board
Clean-up
Double-gated
Entrances: 2
Fenced
Grass/dirt
Parking
Restroom
Seating
Shade structure
Small dog area
Trees
Water

Local Veterinary Clinic

Cote Animal Hospital
San Diego

858-452-7100

Concerns

Flooding

No disabled access

No water in large dog area

Dusty Rhodes Park Dog Park

Sunset Cliffs Blvd.
(between Nimitz &
West Point Loma Blvd.)

This is a large expansive park, with trees all around the sides. The shade is wonderful. And the park was full when we were there—a variety of dogs and people.

Everyone we met was very welcoming. It appeared that all the attendees had great control of their dogs. One favorite was a Yellow Lab that was playing ball, waiting for the throw with his butt in the air and his focus unbreakable.

The community is quite involved in this park, raising money to expand it.

Amenities

Clean-up
Disabled access
Double-gated
Entrances: 2
Fenced
Grass/dirt
Parking
Restroom
Seating
Trees
Water

Concerns

Busy street

No small dog area

The perimeter of park was not clean of dog waste

Local Veterinary Clinic

Sunset Cliffs Animal Hospital, Inc.
San Diego

619-224-0773

Kearney Mesa Dog Park

3170 Armstrong Street

Kearney Mesa has a very active dog park group, with a yahoo-groups list. It also has several sponsors as evidenced by business banners attached to the fencing all around.

The people here were very welcoming and eager to tell the story of their park.

There is no small dog area, and many small dogs were in this park, but many were getting chased by the large dogs—an unsafe situation in any park. Some people explained they hope to put in a separate area for the little guys.

We will return when there is a small dog area. I liked it here.

Special Hours: Closed Thursday am

Local Veterinary Clinic

Cote Animal Hospital
San Diego

858-452-7100

Amenities

Bulletin board
Clean-up
Double-gated
Entrances: 2
Fenced
Grass/dirt
Lights
Parking
Restroom
Seating
Trees
Water

Concerns

Flooding

No small dog area

No disabled access

Maddox Park Dog Park

7815 Flanders Drive
(at Dabney Drive)

Unfortunately this little park has no small dog area, and it appeared that the folks who were at the park when we were there remained somewhat complacent about watching their dogs, and I witnessed several scuffles.

The shade is a future idea, as the trees are quite young yet. The people in the park were nice and courteous to me, but I did make the decision not to take Twyla inside the gate.

The park that the dog area is in is a very pretty park.

Amenities

Clean-up
Disabled access
Double-gated
Entrances: 2
Fenced
Grass/dirt
Seating
Trees
Water

Concerns

No small dog area

No restroom

Local Veterinary Clinic

Rancho Mesa Animal Hospital
San Diego

858-566-0422

Nobel Dog Park

8810 Judicial Drive

A sweet little park with lots of charm, and a huge following. When we visited it was full of small dogs in the small area, but no dogs in the large dog area. When we were leaving, there were no dogs in the small dog area and several in the large area.

GREAT community—the people were friendly to both Twyla and me, as well as each other. We stayed a long time because we enjoyed it. Twyla got to race with a Brussels Griffon named Samson. I score this in my top ten.

Special Hours: Closed Tues. and Thurs.—Large dog closed 9:30-11 am, small dog closed from 11-12:30

Local Veterinary Clinic

Cote Animal Hospital
San Diego

858-452-7100

Amenities

Bulletin board
Clean-up
Disabled access
Double-gated
Entrances: 1
Fenced
Grass/dirt
Lights
Parking
Small dog area
Trees
Water

Concerns

No seating

No restroom

No shade—trees are too young

Shared staging

Rancho Bernardo Off-leash Park

18448 W. Bernardo Drive

This large park has three distinct areas —the middle one closed for maintenance at our visit. It is completely closed in the rain.

There are beautiful adobe benches all throughout with dedication plaques on them. However, I was disappointed at how messy the walkway was with dog poop. It didn't seem to fit the groomed and clean park areas.

The community here is quite social with each other, but not much reaching out to others when I was there.

Special Hours: Closed Thursday am

Local Veterinary Clinic

Companion Care
Veterinary Hospital
San Diego

858-451-0990

Amenities

Bulletin board
Clean-up
Disabled access
Double-gated
Entrances: 3
Fenced
Grass/dirt
Parking
Restroom
Seating
Small dog area
Trees
Water

Concerns

Flooding

Rattlesnake area

Asphalt walkway from the parking lot is quite messy with old (and new) dog poop

No restroom

Torrey Highlands Dog Park

Lansdale Drive
(inside Torrey Highlands Park)

This is a pretty park, very clean and kept well-groomed. The weather was a bit damp on our visit, and the few folks that were using the park were somewhat isolated from each other.

Large and open, but no small dog area available. Eucalyptus trees abound. The bulletin board is surrounded by commemorative bricks and dedications to people and dogs. Appears to be a lot of community involvement here.

I'd like to return to this park at peak time in good weather—my guess is it's a welcoming area.

Amenities

Bulletin board
Clean-up
Disabled access
Double-gated
Entrances: 1
Fenced
Grass/dirt/chips
Parking
Restroom
Seating
Trees
Water

Concerns

Entrance to park is difficult to find

No small dog area

Local Veterinary Clinic

Veterinary Specialty Hospital
San Diego

858-875-7500

San Francisco County

Eureka Valley Dog Run

Collingwood Street & 18th Street
(inside Eureka Valley Rec. Center)

Trying to find a parking place at this park is next to impossible, so mostly it is used by locals. Maintained by the users, this park has a great community of people and neighbors that have become friends.

When it's wet, the gravel is quite urine aromatic. It is a sharp gravel substrate that can be hard on dog paws, as evidenced by Twyla's limp and torn pad when we left.

Barren and plain, this park is not beautiful, but it fits the bill for a city dog.

Special Hours: 6 am-10 pm

Local Veterinary Clinic

Pets Unlimited
San Francisco

415-563-6700

Amenities

Clean-up
Disabled access
Double-gated
Entrances: 2
Fenced
Gravel
Lights
Restroom
Seating
Water

Concerns

Flooding and stinky when wet

No shade

No small dog area

Water outside park

Gates are locked at night by local police

Golden Gate Park Dog Run

In Golden Gate Park
across from the Bison Pasture

This park is located in the beautiful expansive park that is the pride of San Francisco. There are museums, a lake, fields for playing, equine areas, and a Bison field.

The dog park is set far back in the park, and is crowned by huge trees that provide lots of shade. I was hoping for a small dog area but found none.

There were several professional dog walkers when I was there, with numerous dogs, so control of dogs was an issue—some growly behavior that was ignored by handlers. Apparently there are fewer groups present in the evenings. I like this park, it's very pretty and has great running room.

Amenities

Clean-up
Dirt
Double-gated
Entrances: 1
Fenced
Trees
Water

Concerns

Flooding

No small dog area

Disabled access questionable

Local Veterinary Clinic

Pets Unlimited
San Francisco

415-563-6700

St. Mary's Park Dog Park

Justin Dr. & Benton Street

Beautiful lawn area—green and shady with huge trees. A great running area for any dog that needs to stretch out.

It is a bit challenging to find, and the park area was under construction when I visited. To get to this hidden park, you must go down the hill past the playground and the tennis courts.

It can get very mushy in the rain, so the park is closed in wet weather.

Well worth the trek down the hill, and possibly the trek up the hill. Liked this park. Nice folks there.

Special Hours: Closed Friday am

Local Veterinary Clinic

Pets Unlimited
San Francisco

415-563-6700

Amenities

Clean-up
Entrances: 1
Fenced
Grass/asphalt
Lights
Seating
Trees
Water

Concerns

No double-gate

No disabled access

No restroom

No small dog area

Flooding

Challenging to find

Dog can go out of sight of owner

163

Upper Noe Dog Park (Joby's Play Area)

Day Street & Sanchez Street

Very nice mid-city park—lots of people and dogs use this area daily. Great neighborhood, and the people were very friendly and welcoming.

The Day Street entrance is unusual—the park gate is at the street, and the staging entry is a long walkway filled with trees along the long side of the softball field. Beautiful area to play with your dog.

A gentleman named Joby was instrumental in the park's start and visited frequently. He has since passed away and the park carries his name.

Special Hours: Closed Friday am

Amenities

Clean-up
Disabled access
Double-gated
Entrances: 2
Fenced
Gravel/Asphalt
Lights
Seating
Trees
Water

Concerns

No small dog area

No restroom

Local Veterinary Clinic

Pets Unlimited
San Francisco

415-563-6700

Walter Haas Playground Dog Park

Diamond Heights & Addison Street

A park that is in a nice neighborhood but doesn't reflect it. Barren, cold and windy. The fencing is netted to cut down on the chill breeze.

The gravel can be sharp on dog paws. This park is quite popular with dog walkers. There are often many dogs for each walker, so control has been an issue, according to a few individual regulars.

The people we met in this park were very friendly and welcoming, but we didn't stay long after I noticed Twyla was standing in the cold with her tail under, clearly not enjoying herself.

Amenities

Clean-up
Disabled access
Double-gated
Entrances: 1
Fenced
Dirt/gravel
Seating
Water

Concerns

No shade

No small dog area

Gravel tough on dog paws

Can be very cold and windy

No restroom

Local Veterinary Clinic

Pets Unlimited
San Francisco

415-563-6700

San Joaquin County

Kiwanis Bark Park

Lake Park Avenue &
Monterey Park Court

An absolute favorite! This is a wonderfully designed park. The large and small dog areas are separated by a beautifully landscaped walkway. Both of the parks are chock full of playful and whimsical agility and play equipment. And there is a small statue at the entrance at each side, a cement dog waiting to greet you.

Clean, inviting, and green. I loved this park, and wished I had more time to play.

Get to this park whenever you are in the area. Top ten!

Special Hours: Closed Saturday 8-10 am

Local Veterinary Clinic

Country Oaks Veterinary Hospital
Galt

209-745-3200

Amenities

Agility equipment
Bulletin board
Clean-up
Disabled access
Double-gated
Entrances: 2
Fenced
Grass/asphalt
Lights
Parking
Play structure
Restroom
Seating
Small dog area
Trees
Water

Concerns

No shade—very young trees

Allow time to play

Beckman Dog Park

1426 W. Century Blvd.

NOTE: *These two parks are in the same city and are so alike that they are combined here—descriptions are the same, just different addresses.*

Vinewood Dog Park
1824 West Tokay Street
(behind the building,
at Virginia and Stevens Way)

These parks are in sump areas and are pretty unremarkable. They each have, however, a HUGE grassy area that is completely fenced, with beautiful tall redwoods encircling each park.

Due to recent rains, the grass was quite soggy and muddy. Even the signs outside the gates warn of flooding.

Decent areas if your dog needs to stretch out. They are wide and open.

Local Veterinary Clinic

Lodi Veterinary Hospital
Lodi

608-592-3232

Amenities

Clean-up
Entrances: 2
Fenced
Grass/dirt
Seating
Trees

Concerns

Busy street

Flooding

No small dog area

No restroom

No water

No double gate

No disabled access

Barkleyville Dog Park

5505 Feather River Drive

This park has three separate areas: large dog, small dog and agility!

The small dog area has a big, wonderful and whimsical statue of several large dog collars with tags. The large dog area is open, large and great for running. The agility area has everything you could want in play equipment. Twyla and I tried out everything .

Clean, well groomed but a little muddy from recent rain. Appealing. We will return to this one.

Amenities

Agility equipment
Bulletin board
Clean-up
Disabled access
Double-gated
Entrances: 3
Fenced
Grass/gravel & asphalt
Lights
Parking
Play structure
Seating
Small dog area
Trees
Water

Local Veterinary Clinic

Animal Clinic
Stockton

209-477-4853

Concerns

No restroom

Shared staging area

Cora K-9 Facility Dog Park

Kavanagh and Louise Avenues
(in El Pescadero Park)

This is a fun park, with agility equipment and a fire hydrant.

When we visited there was a small gathering, including a couple of young Boxers, a large Pit Bull and a Corgi-mix. After ignoring the advances of the Boxers, Twyla ran and played with the Corgi and Pit Bull.

A pretty park, with some trees and some open grassy area. Great for big dog running, but we watched for prey-drive while they played. Safety, folks! We will return!

Amenities

Agility equipment
Bulletin board
Clean-up
Disabled access
Double-gated
Entrances: 1
Fenced
Fire Hydrants
Grass
Lights
Parking
Restroom
Seating
Trees
Water

Local Veterinary Clinic

Tracy Veterinary Clinic
Tracy

209-835-0626

Concerns

No small dog area

Very breezy

San Luis Obispo County

Elm Street Off-leash Dog Park

Fair Oaks Avenue & Elm Street
(inside Elm Street Park)

This park, while we weren't able to get there ourselves, is in the birthing stages—ready May 2009. There are amenities to be added in the coming year (see Concerns, below), and labor pains will occur for the first year of any new dog park.

For now, provide your own dog bowl and chair if you need to sit.

The local community (Five Cities Dog Park Association) is extremely active here, and the outcome of that effort is looking wonderful! Great people. Lots of pride mixed with sweat and love has gone into this park. Can't wait to take Twyla to the small dog area!

Amenities

Clean-up
Disabled access
Double-gated
Entrances: 3
Fenced
Grass
Parking
Restroom
Small dog area
Trees
Water

Concerns

Shade structure is planned

Seating planned

More trees are planned

Local Veterinary Clinic

Primary Care Dog & Cat Hospital
Arroyo Grande

805-489-4307

El Chorro Regional Dog Park

Hwy. 1— across from
entrance to Cuesta College

This is one of my favorite parks. I even visited twice in one weekend. I met the woman who organized the park. As she entered, she was flocked by all the park dogs—she is clearly a favorite there for everyone.

ALL the people were really nice—a family atmosphere. Picnic tables abound under the pergola, however BBQ pits in the park are cause for concern—eating in a dog park, food aggression between dogs and owners possibly not paying attention to the dogs at all times while socializing.

I liked it here. We'll be back!

Amenities

Bulletin board
Chips
Clean-up
Disabled access
Double-gated
Entrances: 2
Fenced
Parking
Restroom
Seating
Shade structure
Small dog area
Trees
Water

Local Veterinary Clinic

Edna Valley Veterinary Clinic
San Luis Obispo

805-541-8246

Concerns

Fee—$ 4

Large bark - hard on small paws

BBQ pit in park

San Mateo County

Ciprianni Dog Park

2525 Buena Vista
(near Monserat)

You can't see this park from the street. It is located down a long winding asphalt path that goes behind the school.

The small dog park is the size of a postage stamp, and imbedded within the large dog park, so you have to walk through the big dogs to get there.

Appears well-used, although empty when we were there mid-week.

The bulletin board advertised businesses but little information on the club: The Belmont Bowser Club.

Amenities

Bulletin board
Clean-up
Double-gated
Entrances: 1
Fenced
Grass/dirt/gravel
Lights
Parking
Seating
Small dog area
Trees
Water

Concerns

Flooding

No restroom

No disabled access

Challenging to find

Small dog area inside large dog area

Local Veterinary Clinic

Camino Real Pet Clinic
Burlingame

650-344-5711

Brisbane Dog Park

50 Park Lane

This medium sized dog area is beautiful! It is decorated with potted plants and trees, garden decorations all around, and a wonderful seating area with tables and umbrellas and lounge chairs. It also contains some children's toys and toddler bicycles. Like someone's well-loved backyard. Inappropriate for a dog park, however.

I would have loved to sit with a book and an iced tea, but that's not what a dog park is for. It's a lovely little area, but with the children, the gaps in the fence, and the decorations, a bumbling adolescent Labrador would have a hey-day—but not safely.

Lovely, and disappointing.

Local Veterinary Clinic

St. Francis Square
Veterinary Hospital
Daly City

650-992-1100

Amenities

Clean-up
Disabled access
Double-gated
Entrances: 2
Fenced
Grass/gravel
Lights
Parking
Restroom
Seating
Trees
Wading pools
Water

Concerns

Foxtails at edges

No small dog area

Very decorative with garden ornaments—dogs can easily ingest harmful objects

Gaps in fencing

Bayside Park Dog Exercise Area

1125 Airport Blvd.

Long and somewhat narrow, this is a great park for a good run. It is predominantly chips and some gravel, with logs and surface dividers dogs can jump over and play on. To access the small dog area, it is best to park on the street instead of entering the park's parking lot.

There is a small fenced "time out" area near the park entrance that is great for dogs that get too wound up or if there is need to give another dog a break.

I really like this park and have been back to it several times. Beautifully landscaped and groomed. Have fun!

Amenities

Bulletin board
Clean-up
Double-gated
Entrances: 2
Fenced
Chips
Restroom
Seating
Small dog area
Trees
Water

Concerns

Next to waste water treatment plant

You can lose sight of your dog

No disabled access

Local Veterinary Clinic

Camino Real Pet Clinic
Burlingame

650-344-5711

Palisades Park Dog Area

100 Palisades Drive

Okay—someone just put up a fence and a double gate and called it a dog area. Perhaps this was an after-thought—so the dog can go somewhere and not be in the way of other park users. I suppose it fills the purpose of taking off the leash, but I see little else. Twyla didn't even sniff much, just looked up at me as if to say "Well…?"

The one great thing about this park is the view, but as I think about it, that's outside of the park.

Amenities

Double-gated
Entrances: 1
Fenced
Grass
Seating

Concerns

No shade

No small dog area

No water

No disabled access

No clean-up

No restroom

Local Veterinary Clinic

St. Francis Square
Veterinary Hospital
Daly City

650-992-1100

Foster City Dog Exercise Area

Foster City Blvd. & Bounty Drive

The atmosphere was very positive and social, and it felt as though it was a lot larger than it really is. Great running space. This park has been recently refurbished.

Busy and full of a great variety of dogs. Reminded me of a summer Saturday afternoon at the neighborhood swimming pool. The dogs were chasing balls and toys as if they were doing cannon-balls from the side of the pool—every dog in their own focused world. It was great fun, and the people appeared to have a good community and decent control of their dogs in all the chaos. We'll be back!

Special Hours: 6 am-10 pm

Local Veterinary Clinic

Animal Cove Pet Hospital
Foster City

650-377-0822

Amenities

Agility equipment
Bulletin board
Clean-up
Disabled access
Double-gated
Entrances: 1
Fenced
Gravel/turf
Lights
Parking
Restroom
Seating
Shade structure
Small dog area
Trees
Water

Concerns

Can be hot—the turf reflects heat although does not get hot on the paws

San Mateo County—Half Moon Bay

Coastside Dog Park

Wavecrest Rd. off Hwy. 1

This park is a bit barren, not sheltered in any way. Being that it is next to the Pacific Ocean, it is quite windy and can be cold and foggy. It is apparently a "semi-permanent" dog area—the landowner has not designated it as permanent yet, after several years. As a result there is a very involved effort to make it so, with plans to improve the area. Even the fencing is temporary.

Given that there is limited access to the beaches, it is a much needed area, and well-used by dog owners in the area. The community I met were very warm and welcoming, and the dogs have lots of room to run.

I shivered a lot but had a good time.

Local Veterinary Clinic

St. Francis Square
Veterinary Hospital
Daly City

650-992-1100

Amenities

Bulletin board
Clean-up
Double-gated
Entrances: 1
Fenced
Chips
Parking
Restroom
Seating
Timeout enclosure

Concerns

No small dog area

No disabled access

Flooding

Very windy

Willow Oaks Park Off-leash Area

Willow Road & Coleman Street

Too bad about the limited hours—this is a very nice little park that has great community support and wonderful people and dogs that attend. All the folks were very warm and welcoming and were anxious to share information about the area.

The main things the folks would like to change: the limited hours, no seating, and the lack of water.

This park is clean and green, with a nice big tree that provides great shade. I will definitely be back here—I really liked it.

Special Hours: 7-9 AM, 4 pm—Dusk

Local Veterinary Clinic

Redwood Pet Hospital
Redwood City

650-366-4180

Amenities

Clean-up
Disabled access
Double-gated
Entrances: 1
Fenced
Grass/dirt
Parking
Tree

Concerns

Did not see restroom

No small dog area

No water

No seating

Very limited hours although not a multi-use area

Flooding

Shores Dog Park

Radio Road near
Redwood Shores Parkway

We arrived at sunrise and were delighted to be accompanied by a flock of ducks and geese on the pond next to the park area. It was peaceful and quiet, and I could see from the surface of the dirt that several dogs had played here on days prior to our visit—skid, run and slide marks.

The small dog area is quite small, but the sniffs, apparently, are the best. A large German Shepherd was in the large dog area, running and chasing balls, and I noticed there was significant dust.

Comfortable and a good relaxing area.

Amenities

Clean-up
Entrances: 2
Fenced
Grass/dirt
Parking
Small dog area
Trees
Water

Concerns

No disabled access

No restroom

No seating

Local Veterinary Clinic

Sequoia Veterinary Hospital
Redwood City

650-369-7326

Commodore Dog Run

Commodore & Cherry

While the small and large dog areas are separate, they are often open to each other unless someone feels their dog is at risk. So I suggest "scoping" it out before entering.

The community here was great—very social and welcoming. All the attendees seemed to know each other, and had very good control of the active and pushy dogs.

This park is clean and well-groomed, and obviously used a lot but monitored well. I had a really good time and we'll be back!

Amenities

Bulletin board
Clean-up
Disabled access
Entrances: 2
Fenced
Grass/dirt/gravel
Parking
Restroom
Seating
Small dog area
Trees
Water

Concerns

No double gates at the entries

Small dog area is often open into large dog area

Local Veterinary Clinic

Spruce Avenue Pet Hospital
South San Francisco

650-873-6880

Seal Point Dog Park

Off 3rd Avenue—Seal Point Area
(inside Shoreline Park)

This very popular park is always busy. It is large and open and is set up for great dog runs. The power poles provide some interrupters and cement surfaces for hopping up and down. The winding gravel walkway extends throughout the park making disabled access quite easy.

The small dog area is a nice size, up against the large dog area, and with an exit either to the parking lot or into the large dog park.

It appears there is some problem in the small area with consistent clean-up, but other than that, it's a great park. We've returned a few times.

Amenities

Bulletin board
Clean-up
Disabled access
Double-gated
Entrances: 3
Fenced
 Gravel
Parking
Restroom
Seating
Shade structure
Small dog area
Water

Concerns

Can be hot, or quite cold and windy

Gravel is rough and can be hard on tender dog paws

No trees

Local Veterinary Clinic

North Peninsula
Veterinary Clinic, Inc.
San Mateo

650-348-2575

Santa Barbara County

WOOF PAC Park

300 Goodwin Road
(inside Waller County Park)

When entering this park at the main entrance, you will walk in through a large red dog-house door.

The people I spoke with were wonderful—there were a few women that meet at the park every day at 2:30 and bring their director chairs with their dog's name on the back ("Ozzie's Mom") so there is no mistaking them.

Both areas are green and open and the dogs love to run. Twyla appeared to love it, I loved it, so it's right up there with the best of them!

Amenities

Bulletin board
Clean-up
Disabled access
Double-gated
Entrances: 4
Fenced
Grass/dirt
Parking
Restroom
Seating
Small dog area
Trees
Water

Local Veterinary Clinic

Santa Maria Animal Hospital
Santa Maria

805-925-4059

Concerns

While I was there, the dogs in the large dog area were not well under control— lots of growl-fests

Santa Clara County

Santa Clara County—Campbell

Los Gatos Creek Park Dog Park

1250 Dell Avenue

There are a large variety of surfaces in this park—one for every taste! There are small boulders and logs placed throughout for more interesting chase-and-play areas. Of course we were there on Monday (they close on Mondays) so we peered longingly through the gate.

The gravel and dirt surfaces were clearly used a lot due to paw prints and skid marks, so we imagined lots of tennis balls. They are VERY strict on the division of large and small dogs for safety purposes, which I was pleased to see.

Great park—we'll be back.

Special Hours: Closed Monday

Local Veterinary Clinic

Central Animal Hospital
Campbell

408-340-7183

Amenities

Bulletin board
Clean-up
Disabled access
Double-gated
Entrances: 1
Fenced
Grass/dirt &
chips/asphalt
Parking
Restroom
Seating
Shade structure
Small dog area
Trees
Water

Concerns

Day-use permit
required - a fee of
$5 for park entry

Milpitas Dog Park

3000 Levin Park Access Road

Beautifully done, this park is a highlight on any dog park map. It is quite clean and well-groomed, and the community appears to be quite involved in the care and maintenance. Nice folks.

The small dog area is filled with shade trees (I counted twelve), and while the large area has few trees, the small dog trees provide shade for both areas.

Twyla met a Beagle, and they ran and ran and played and played. We stayed quite a long time at this park and got more than our $6 fees in fun. We'll be back!

Special Hours: Closed Thursday am

Amenities

Bulletin board
Clean-up
Disabled access
Double-gated
Entrances: 1
Fenced
Grass/dirt/gravel
Restroom
Seating
Small dog area
Trees
Water

Concerns

Permit required - $6 at entry gate

Shared staging

Local Veterinary Clinic

Calaveras Veterinary Clinic
Milpitas

408-262-7200

Morgan Hill Off-leash Dog Park

Edmundson Avenue &
Monterey Street

We arrived at this wonderful park on the day of their 1-year anniversary party. There were a few vendors and all the "officials" of the park.

The community is very involved with this park's maintenance and upkeep. Quite a dedicated group. Twyla and I were welcomed by everyone, and I wish we lived closer! Beautiful rolling hills and plenty of fire hydrants to keep any boy-dog happy.

We'll drop in any time we pass through, and love every minute of it. Can they please have a party every weekend? A top ten fave.

Amenities

Bulletin board
Clean-up
Disabled access
Double-gated
Entrances: 1
Fenced
Grass/dirt
Parking
Restroom
Seating
Small dog area
Trees
Water

Concerns

Large dog area has some areas where your dog is not always visible

Darn, they don't have a party every weekend

Local Veterinary Clinic

Animal Care Center
Morgan Hill

408-779-4010

Mountain View Dog Park

North Shoreline Blvd.
at Bill Graham Parkway

This is a great park—very good community and warm welcomes during our visit.

Most people were responsible about their dog's behavior but there were a few that seemed complacent as they were deep in conversation.

A Labrador puppy caught Twyla's fancy so this is one of her favorites. However, some of the individual regulars tell me multi-dog walkers sort of take over the park at certain times, so some users avoid the park at that time. I had a good time, and will be back!

Amenities

Bulletin board
Clean-up
Disabled access
Double-gated
Entrances: 1
Fenced
Dirt
Parking
Restroom
Seating
Shade structure
Small dog area
Trees
Water

Concerns

Used by multi-dog walkers, many don't use the park during the daytime when the dog walkers are there

Local Veterinary Clinic

Miramonte Veterinary Hospital
Mountain View

650-962-8338

Greer Park—Pup 'n Run

1098 Amarillo

Am I on "Candid Camera?!" Maybe we missed something, but when Twyla and I went into this (empty) park, Twyla looked up at me with that "Where's the park?" look, and I could only shrug.

This park is as small and basic as it can be. It looks as though someone charted out a few feet of grass under a tree, set up a short cyclone fence, and called it a dog park.

It was clean. And I didn't notice any messes left by previous users... were there previous users?

Special Hours: 7 am-4:30 pm

Local Veterinary Clinic

El Camino Animal Hospital
Palo Alto

650-326-1211

Amenities

Disabled access
Entrances: 2
Fenced
Grass
Parking
Restroom
Trees

Concerns

Flooding

No small dog area

No water

No seating

No double gates

Hoover Park

Cowper Street &
Loma Verde Avenue

I don't often use the word "charming" but that was my first thought when I arrived at this small park.

Located near a waterway, it was pleasant and cool here. The people were quite welcoming and invited me directly into their social group. Had I had more time, I would have stayed all afternoon.

The community keeps this park well-groomed and clean. This one goes near the top of the list, and we will be back. Soon.

Amenities

Clean-up
Double-gated
Entrances: 2
Fenced
Dirt/chips
Restroom
Seating
Trees
Water

Concerns

No small dog area

No disabled access

Fence is barely
3 feet tall

Local Veterinary Clinic

El Camino Animal Hospital
Palo Alto

650-326-1211

Mitchell Dog Run

600 East Meadow
(inside J. Pearce Mitchell Park)

You can find this dog area behind the tennis courts inside the park. There were a few people there, and they didn't notice new people or dogs entering the park. From what I was told, it isn't always like that, and regulars can be quite social.

Full of a lot of sand, so watch for some dust when the dogs get a good run going.

Not an exceptional park, but Twyla had some fun with other small dogs. I look forward to coming back and meeting the "regulars."

Amenities

Bulletin board
Clean-up
Double-gated
Entrances: 1
Fenced
Grass/dirt/gravel
Lights
Parking
Restroom
Seating
Shade structure
Trees
Water

Concerns

No disabled access

No small dog area

Local Veterinary Clinic

El Camino Animal Hospital
Palo Alto

650-326-1211

Butcher Park Dog Park

3050 Camden Avenue &
Lancaster Drive

While we were staying in San Jose to cover the parks in the area, everyone at other parks told us about Butcher. Since we slept nearby, we visited the park 3 times in 2 days. It is one of the top ten in my book.

Great people! The community is strong, and fun. Everybody, even the puppy tails, were smiling.

Very secure. Wonderful landscaping, green and shady. I wish we could visit this park every day. We will be back!

Amenities

Bulletin board
Clean-up
Disabled access
Double-gated
Entrances: 1
Fenced
Turf/dirt/gravel
Parking
Restroom
Seating
Small dog area
Trees
Water

Concerns

Lots of little children when we visited

While turf is a great idea, it had a bit of an odor

Local Veterinary Clinic

Bascom Animal Hospital
Campbell

408-796-6749

Delmas Dog Park

Park Avenue & Delmas Avenue

_____

Even though this nice little park is situated right next to a light rail track, the approach is so quiet that Twyla never even looked up.

One block long, and not terribly wide, this is a great park for a decent run. There is a gravel walkway along the inside of the fence for the entire block distance, all of which is disabled accessible.

The people here were very nice, social and kept the park extremely clean. I liked it very much, and will return.

Amenities

Clean-up
Disabled access
Double-gated
Entrances: 1
Fenced
Dirt/gravel
Lights
Parking
Seating
Trees
Water

Concerns

No small dog area

No restroom

Next to a light rail so be careful when crossing the street

Some bushes, can lose sight of your dog briefly

Local Veterinary Clinic

Bascom Animal Hospital
Campbell

408-796-6749

Fontana Dog Park

Golden Oak Way
(inside Jeffrey Fontana Park)

This is a wonderful neighborhood park off the beaten path. The neighborhood and park users have supplied many chairs of all varieties for our comfort.

I love the location of the water fountain, far from the entrance gates—makes for less crowding and rushing at the gate.

The people are very social, and I was told that it never gets terribly crowded at one time but has a large following.

I had a great time, and would love to return to this park!

Special Hours: Closed Tuesday and some Fridays

Local Veterinary Clinic

Story Road Animal Hospital
San Jose

408-292-6600

Amenities

Clean-up
Disabled access
Double-gated
Entrances: 2
Fenced
Dirt/gravel
Parking
Restroom
Seating
Small dog area
Trees
Water

Concerns

Sometimes the maintenance gate at the far end is left open

Didn't see the restrooms, but the park is pretty big

Hellyer Park Dog Run

985 Hellyer Avenue
(inside Hellyer Regional Park)

This is a large park with plenty of room to run. When we visited this park for the first time, there happened to be a gathering of Lab and Goldendoodles. You could say there were Oodles of Doodles.

The people in this park were warm, wonderful and welcoming and eager to share the park's history.

Lots of shade trees, and green grass. The dog run is up at the end of the road at the top of the hill past the fee kiosk. When can we go back?

Special Hours: Closed Wednesday

Local Veterinary Clinic

Bascom Animal Hospital
Campbell

408-796-6749

Amenities

Bulletin board
Clean-up
Disabled access
Double-gated
Entrances: 1
Fenced
Grass/dirt/chips
Parking
Restroom
Seating
Trees
Water

Concerns

Permit required—
Fee: $6

Closed during rainy weather

No small dog area

Miyuki Dog Park

Miyuki Drive (at dead end)

I really liked this park—it is only about a year old, beautifully groomed and clean, replacing another older dog park in this area. The water pressure in the fountain is extremely weak. The gate latch was broken so it was rigged with a bungee cord. The staging area had some gaps that a very small dog could slip through.

The people here were wonderful—kind and warm and helpful. They told us about the park's history.

This is one of my favorites. I think I see Twyla wagging as I write.

Amenities

Bulletin board
Clean-up
Disabled access
Double-gated
Entrances: 1
Fenced
Grass/dirt/gravel
Parking
Restroom
Seating
Shade structure
Small dog area
Trees
Water

Local Veterinary Clinic

Story Road Animal Hospital
San Jose

408-292-6600

Concerns

Recessed tree trunks—a hazard for running dogs

Gate latch broken when we visited

Ryland Dog Park

North First & Ryland Park Drive

This ornate little park is directly under Coleman Ave overpass. The wrought iron fence has decorative dog silhouettes all around. The paw prints in the gravel indicate it is used. Kind of barren and plain inside the park.

The gravel was tough on Twyla's feet, and a good run scraped her pads raw. When we visited it was a warm Saturday afternoon, and I was surprised it was empty. The overpass provides good shade.

This park did not excite me, although the fencing was beautiful.

Amenities

Bulletin board
Clean-up
Double-gated
Entrances: 1
Fenced
Gravel
Seating
Water

Concerns

Disabled access challenging with the gravel

No small dog area

Small dogs could easily escape under the fence

Gravel very rough

No restroom

Local Veterinary Clinic

Bascom Animal Hospital
Campbell

408-796-6749

Saratoga Creek Park

End of Graves Avenue
(behind Orchard Supply Hardware)

This is a sweet park. Shady and cool on hot days, the trees also provide some protection from the rain on wet days.

The community in this park appeared very strong and connected. There was a lot of interaction between people in an inclusive manner. I was warmly welcomed. Not only were they interactive with other people, but everybody loved-up every other dog as well.

This is a very active park, and we will return to enjoy this location again.

Amenities

Bulletin board
Clean-up
Disabled access
Double-gated
Entrances: 2
Fenced
Turf/dirt/chips
Parking
Restroom
Seating
Trees
Water

Concerns

No small dog area

Was a little tricky to find

Local Veterinary Clinic

Story Road Animal Hospital
San Jose

408-292-6600

Watson Dog Park

550 N. 22nd Street

This park is large and barren, and can be very hot. Only one large group of trees right in the center where everyone was huddled when we arrived.

To go from the gravel lot to the park you must walk through a beat-up weedy area marked with all kinds of cautions due to toxic soil. Word is that this park will be destroyed, with no replacement in mind.

With all the warning signs, I was not anxious to visit this park. We stayed a very short time.

Special Hours: 7 am-10 pm

Local Veterinary Clinic

Story Road Animal Hospital
San Jose

408-292-6600

Amenities

Clean-up
Double-gated
Entrances: 2
Fenced
Grass/dirt
Restroom
Seating
Small dog area
Trees
Water

Concerns

Foxtails

No shade in small dog area

No disabled access

Built on an old toxic dump site

Reed Street Dog Park

888 Reed Street

The community is quite active in the park as far as improvements and input on use. While there, I was told that the small dog area was new and they were trying to get it enlarged. Apparently it can get quite crowded.

The grassy mound in the center of the park is great for running and chasing, but it is slippery for people in the rain, and the mounds are tall enough that you can lose sight of your dog.

Liked the people, and the park is pretty. Looking forward to seeing the improvements the community makes.

Special Hours: Closed Thursday

Local Veterinary Clinic

Animal Clinic
Santa Clara

408-241-8200

Amenities

Bulletin board
Clean-up
Disabled access
Double-gated
Entrances: 2
Fenced
Grass/gravel
Parking
Restroom
Seating
Shade structure
Small dog area
Trees
Water

Concerns

Trees are very young

Small hills in center of each area can be quite slippery when wet

Las Palmas Park Dog Park

850 Russett Drive

Just inside the gate of this park is an inlay in stone of a dog's profile. The fence is slated cyclone which cuts down on fence rushing as the inside dogs are unable to see if a dog is entering. The benches, water and "social" areas are far from the gate, which is also a nice safety feature. The trees inside the park are surrounded by fencing, which keeps running dog feet out of the recessed base of the trees.

The community in this park was wonderful. They welcomed us as newcomers, eager to engage us in conversation.

I liked this park.

Special Hours: 8 am-8 pm (Caution: auto lock gate)

Local Veterinary Clinic

ELC Veterinary Clinic
Sunnyvale

408-737-2333

Amenities

Bulletin board
Clean-up
Double-gated
Entrances: 1
Fenced
Dirt/gravel
Parking
Restroom
Seating
Trees
Water

Concerns

No small dog area

No disabled access

Hose is inside staging area

Santa Cruz County

Polo Grounds Dog Park

2255 Huntington Avenue
(inside Polo Grounds County Park)

When we visited this park, all of the dogs, big and small, were in the large dog area. There is an area for small dogs available, but apparently it is not used much. It is used regularly for shy, elderly or more aggressive dogs.

The atmosphere in the park was welcoming, and the people were very social with each other, and with me when we entered.

The large dog area is quite big, so dogs can really get a good run. Nice park. I liked it, and wish there was more use of the small dog area.

Amenities

Bulletin board
Clean-up
Disabled access
Double-gated
Entrances: 2
Fenced
Chips
Parking
Restroom
Seating
Shade structure
Small dog area
Trees
Water

Local Veterinary Clinic

Aptos-Creekside Pet Hospital
Aptos

831-688-4242

Concerns

Trees are outside the perimeter of the park, so shade is minimal

Scotts Valley Dog Park

1 Civic Center Drive
(inside Sky Park)

I liked this park a lot. Twyla had one particular admirer—a little Maltese named Joey, that followed her faithfully during our entire time there.

The small dog area and the large dog area can be opened and combined to create one large park.

The people in this park are quite friendly and welcoming. I was told that this park may be relocating, and that the "wheels of politics" turn slowly.

We look forward to visiting this park again!

Amenities

Bulletin board
Clean-up
Disabled access
Double-gated
Entrances: 2
Fenced
Dirt/chips/gravel
Parking
Restroom
Seating
Shade structure
Small dog area
Wading pool
Water

Local Veterinary Clinic

Mt. Hermon Veterinary Clinic
Scotts Valley

831-438-0803

Concerns

No trees

Can be hot and dry

Watsonville Dog Park

757 Green Valley Road
(inside Pinto Lake County Park)

It was a Sunday afternoon and this
park was empty when we arrived. It
does, however, look to be well-used as
evidenced by the paw prints and skid
marks in the dirt.

It isn't fancy, by any means; it is fairly
plain. I had to be careful of the many
poison oak plants that surrounded the
perimeter of the park just outside the
fence. The rattlesnake warnings kept
me looking and watching wherever
Twyla wandered and sniffed.

This park is basic and fills a need.

Amenities

Clean-up
Disabled access
Double-gated
Entrances: 1
Fenced
Dirt/chips
Parking
Restroom
Seating
Small dog area
Trees
Water

Concerns

Rattlesnake area

Poison oak

Local Veterinary Clinic

Animal Hospital of Watsonville
Watsonville

831-728-1439

Shasta County

Redding Dog Park—Benton Park

Placer Street & Airport Park Drive

This is a wonderful park, with great community. We visited twice while we were in town. Our drive was long to get there and worth every minute.

This group is quite active, holding events several times a year at the park. Regulars were eager to talk about their involvement in special events and clean-up "parties."

After dark, the lights are coin-operated: four quarters will light the park for a full hour. I loved this park and would drive far and wide to visit again.

Special Hours: 6 am-10 pm

Local Veterinary Clinic

Redding Veterinary Clinic
Redding

530-243-8335

Amenities

Bulletin board
Clean-up
Disabled access
Double-gated
Entrances: 3
Fenced
Grass/dirt
Lights
Parking
Seating
Small dog area
Trees
Water

Concerns

No restroom

Next to a small plane airport—planes fly low and may startle a shy or timid dog

Solano County

Phoenix Community Dog Park

Rose Drive & Kearney Drive

Other than the fact that it was a bit challenging to find at first, this is a nice park.

It is a large wide open area, with numerous shade trees. There is, however, a dog training class that happens in the small dog area every Monday from 5:00-6:30 pm— unfortunately right at prime time for people and dogs visiting the park.

When we were there, there were a few dog-squabbles, but the people were great at intervening. I will return here.

Amenities

Bulletin board
Clean-up
Disabled access
Double-gated
Entrances: 2
Fenced
Grass/dirt
Parking
Seating
Small dog area
Trees
Water

Concerns

No restroom

Park is way back off of dirt road, past the skate-board park

Muddy in center

Local Veterinary Clinic

Southampton Pet Hospital Ltd.
Benicia

707-745-1135

Solano County—Vacaville

Vacaville Dog Park

Pena Adobe & Hwy. I80
(inside Lagoon Valley Park)

This park appears to have several names depending on who you ask: Vacaville Dog Park, Lagoon Valley Dog Park, Janine Jordan Park.

The setting is nice, lots of trees with lagoon. Only a few folks there when we visited, but the park looks well used. A lot of nice shade trees. On our first visit, the park was closed for maintenance on a Saturday.

It was a warm summer day. Lots of bugs in the air—gnats, I think—getting in my face, eyes and mouth. We left early.

Local Veterinary Clinic

VACA Valley Veterinary Hospital
Vacaville

707-446-0466

Amenities

Bulletin board
Clean-up
Disabled access
Double-gated
Entrances: 1
Fenced
Grass/dirt
Parking
Seating
Trees
Water

Concerns

No small dog area

Permit required—$3 fee to enter the park

Did not see any restroom

Very windy and lots of flying bugs

Wardlaw Dog Park

1805 Ascot Parkway
(inside Wardlaw Park)

This park is part of the Greater Vallejo Recreation District.

Even given the concerns listed below, I found this to be a nice park. The folks there were very warm and welcoming, and it was evident that there is a strong community there.

Lots of running room for the big dogs, although the small dog area is quite a bit smaller.

The park is very green and clean. I liked it here.

Amenities

Bulletin board
Clean-up
Disabled access
Entrances: 1
Fenced
Grass/dirt
Parking
Restroom
Seating
Small dog area
Water

Concerns

No shade

Many owners appeared to have little control of their dogs during our visit

Lots of young people with bikes and skateboards

Local Veterinary Clinic

Redwood Veterinary Hospital
Vallejo

707-553-1400

Sonoma County

Helen Putnam Park

Myrtle Avenue & Macklin Drive

The park surrounding the dog park is very nice. This compact dog area is behind the softball field.

This is a strange little area. Very tiny fenced area with one single gate at the entrance, but on the back side of the little square are two open backyards that each have their own broken down gates into the dog area.

The park was not appealing in the least and it may have actually been the first dog park we didn't want to go in. Use it if you're desperate.

Amenities

Clean-up
Entrances: 1
Fenced
Grass
Parking
Restroom
Seating
Water

Concerns

Flooding

Foxtails

Weeds

No shade

No small dog area

No water

No disabled access

Local Veterinary Clinic

La Plaza Veterinary Clinic
Cotati

707-794-1299

Elizabeth Anne Perrone Dog Park

13630 Sonoma Highway
(inside Sonoma Valley
Regional Park)

A nice park. Big and green, with a small gazebo and some random agility equipment.

It is well-used, and kept very clean. There weren't many people at the park when we visited but those that were there were very welcoming.

Tables and chairs were clustered in a variety of areas as though groups of people were gathered.

This park is a good one. Too bad there is no small dog area.

Amenities

Agility equipment
Clean-up
Double-gated
Entrances: 2
Fenced
Grass/dirt
Parking
Restroom
Seating
Shade structure
Trees
Water

Local Veterinary Clinic

Glen Ellen Veterinary Hospital
Glen Ellen

707-996-2300

Concerns

No small dog area

Fee: $5

No disabled access

Badger Dog Park

750 Heron Drive
(inside Badger Park)

This park is for small dogs under 25 pounds only. This is a fun rough and tumble area! The dogs were having a great time running and wrestling, and Twyla joined right in.

Very clean, lots of shade and a welcoming community that obviously knew each other well. People apparently travel from outlying areas to visit here, even with other parks situated closer to them.

The neighbors must love the sound wall that shields them from the happy yaps! I loved this park.

Amenities

Bulletin board
Clean-up
Double-gated
Entrances: 2
Fenced
Grass/chips
Parking
Seating
Small dog area
Trees
Water

Concerns

No area for dogs larger than 25 pounds

No disabled access

No restroom

Local Veterinary Clinic

Redwood Veterinary Clinic
Santa Rosa

707-542-4012

Villa Chanticleer Dog Park

1248 Chanticleer Way

Nice park with two levels. The staging area is the size of a small dog park in itself, then you go up some stairs to the top level, and voila! there's the park.

The upper level has some great oak trees that provide the shade that only an oak tree can provide, and a water fountain area with wading pools.

The people there were very welcoming and enjoyed talking about their dogs and experiences in the park.

I will be back!

Amenities

Bulletin board
Clean-up
Double-gated
Entrances: 1
Fenced
Chips
Parking
Restroom
Seating
Shade structure
Trees
Wading pools
Water

Local Veterinary Clinic

Redwood Veterinary Clinic
Santa Rosa

707-542-4012

Concerns

No small dog area

Rattlesnake area

No disabled access

Rocky Memorial Dog Park

Casa Grande near Lakeville

Drive slowly to the parking area—it is INSIDE the dog park. As a result the driveway area is not fenced.

This is a huge expanded grassy hilly area for dogs to really run and play. I was amazed at how many acres it encompassed! The social groups, however, were very small and quite isolated—I am not sure if that was due to the size of the park or the community itself.

This would not be the place to take a dog that runs and runs without a good recall. There's entirely too much area.

Amenities

Clean-up
Disabled access
Entrances: 1
Partially fenced
Grass/dirt
Parking
Restroom
Seating
Water

Concerns

Flooding

Foxtails

No shade

No small dog area

It is easy to lose track of your dog

Partial fencing

Local Veterinary Clinic

East Petaluma Animal Hospital
Petaluma

707-765-9098

Field of Friends

7469 Bernice Avenue

This is a two-cents plain little grassy area behind a ball field. Very few amenities.

The trees surrounding the outside of the back fence are very pretty and can be somewhat shady if the sun is not directly overhead.

There is no seating, and no water. It is impeccably clean of garbage and dog leavings. The grass is wonderfully plush.

Twyla and I were alone in the park, on a weekend day. Usually a time when the parks are busiest.

Amenities

Bulletin board
Clean-up
Double-gated
Entrances: 1
Fenced
Grass/dirt
Lights
Parking
Restroom

Concerns

Flooding

No seating

No disabled access

No small dog area

No water

Trees are outside the park

Local Veterinary Clinic

North Park Veterinary Clinic
Rohnert Park

707-585-2899

Rohnert Park Dog Park

Robert's Lake Road
(next to Golf Course)

This wonderful park is chock-full of willow trees for shade. It was hot on the day we visited, and the trees were a welcome sight.

It is very long, and dogs can get a great run going. The small dog area was significantly smaller but green and shady.

The community of users we met was very friendly and social, and all owners appeared to have excellent control over their dogs. Glad to have visited here!

Special Hours: Closed Monday until 10 am

Local Veterinary Clinic

North Park Veterinary Clinic
Rohnert Park

707-585-2899

Amenities

Bulletin board
Clean-up
Double-gated
Entrances: 2
Fenced
Grass/dirt/chips
Seating
Small dog area
Trees
Water

Concerns

Next to freeway

Flying golf balls could be an issue

No restroom

No disabled access

Shelter Park

301 J. Rogers Lane
(at Rohnert Park Animal Control)

This can be a little challenging to find. It is located deep behind industrial businesses adjacent to a small Animal Control building.

The hours can also be prohibitive. They were closed up when we arrived for our visit. The hours are very limited.

Very small area, clearly used a lot by shelter dogs. My concern is that the cleanliness may not be ideal for disease control. The toys in the park are worn and shaggy. Many of the dogs that play here are living in the shelter.

Special Hours: Only dawn-9 am, and 5 pm-dark

Local Veterinary Clinic

North Park Veterinary Clinic
Rohnert Park

707-585-2899

Amenities

Bulletin board
Clean-up
Double-gated
Entrances: 1
Fenced
Chips/gravel
Parking
Restroom
Seating
Shade structure
Water

Concerns

Flooding

Open to the public very limited time

Concerns about infection control

No small dog area

No disabled access

Doyle Park Dog Park

698 Doyle Park Drive
(inside Doyle Park)

The small dog area can be created by closing a gate between the park areas. However, it is usually left open.

Very social people with their dogs. Lots of huge trees make it feel like a camping area. All dogs were together in the large joined areas. We stayed a long time here. Twyla found some good buddies, and some leftover energy from somewhere.

Dogs appear to love this park as evidenced by their racing, chasing, wrestling and playing.

Amenities

Clean-up
Disabled access
Entrances: 4
Fenced
Grass/dirt/chips
Parking
Restroom
Seating
Small dog area
Trees
Water

Concerns

Flooding

Foxtails

Not double gated

Small dogs can get out under the fence (one dog came IN the park that way)

Local Veterinary Clinic

Redwood Veterinary Clinic
Santa Rosa

707-542-4012

227

DeTurk Round Barn Park

819 Donahue Street
(AKA: Maverick Park)

This is a sweet little neighborhood park nestled among pretty homes. It is green and relaxing, and I almost wanted to grab a book and lay on the grass in the sun. (But I know better about grass in dog parks…). We'd give this one a "jumping dog" reference, but there was really no place to—it was pretty small.

There is a bulletin board and memorial in front of the park, dedicated to a Police K-9 killed in the line of duty.

The people were very nice, and Twyla played with Oso, a wonderful gentleman Staffordshire Terrier.

Amenities

Bulletin board
Clean-up
Disabled access
Entrances: 1
Fenced
Grass/gravel
Seating
Trees
Water

Concerns

No small dog area

Small dogs can escape under fence

No restroom

The white picket fence is only 3 ft. high all around

Local Veterinary Clinic

Redwood Veterinary Clinic
Santa Rosa

707-542-4012

Galvin Dog Park

3330 Yulupa Avenue
(in Don Galvin Park)

Long but narrow park, located behind tennis courts and next to the Bennett Valley Golf Course.

Appears to be well-cared for and used, although it was empty when we visited midday on a weekend. The skid marks in the chips and mulch are evidence that someone had been running and chasing recently.

Beautiful willow trees provide shade, which is great on a hot day. It is a very comfortable setting, and Twyla appeared to enjoy the smells along the fence.

Amenities

Bulletin board
Clean-up
Disabled access
Double-gated
Entrances: 2
Fenced
Grass/chips
Parking
Restroom
Seating
Trees
Water

Concerns

Foxtails are quite prevalent in one area of the park

No small dog area

Slight opening in maintenance gate area—small dog could escape

Local Veterinary Clinic

Redwood Veterinary Clinic
Santa Rosa

707-542-4012

Northwest Community Dog Park

2536 Steele Lane
(in Northwest Community Park)

Unfortunately, this is not a park I would return to. The hazards are too numerous—bees, escape areas in the fence and gate, and the park area is very poorly groomed.

When we were there, a woman had her three small dogs attached to the back fence on 4 foot leads so they could not escape.

I can't even say it fills the bill.

Amenities

Bulletin board
Clean-up
Double-gated
Entrances: 2
Fenced
Grass/dirt/chips
Restroom
Seating
Small dog area
Trees
Wading pools
Water

Concerns

No disabled access

Clover is the ground cover—lots of bees

Easy escape

Water is in a horse trough—small dogs can't reach it

Local Veterinary Clinic

Redwood Veterinary Clinic
Santa Rosa

707-542-4012

Rincon Community Dog Park

5108 Badger Road

This park is the epitome of a warm community gathering place—the people are "neighborly." We met an elderly gentleman who was a retired large-animal veterinarian, and he was training his Kelpie in the park.

The pond is in a third fenced area, outside the two park sections. Very shady and cool in the heat.

The one overwhelming desire of the users is to put in wood chips instead of dirt, to keep the mud down.

This is a favorite.

Amenities

Bulletin board
Clean-up
Disabled access
Double-gated
Entrances: 1
Fenced
Grass/dirt
Parking
Pond to play in
Restroom
Seating
Small dog area
Trees
Water

Concerns

Flooding

Large dog area is closed in winter

Can be quite muddy

Local Veterinary Clinic

Redwood Veterinary Clinic
Santa Rosa

707-542-4012

Ragle Ranch Animal Care Cntr. Dog Park

500 Ragle Road
(in Ragle Ranch Park)

This park was our #100 park visit in our project, so it holds a special place for me.

This is an absolute favorite. A slight hillside for dogs to run up and down, with no areas where the dogs are not visible.

The users are organized in their clean-up days, and special dog events occur throughout the year. They provide gloves, tools and refreshments on clean-up days. The atmosphere is very welcoming and social, and the group has a web-list group that communicates as needed.

Amenities

Bulletin board
Clean-up
Double-gated
Entrances: 1
Fenced
Grass/dirt/chips
Parking
Permit required
Restroom
Seating
Small dogs—
    limited hours
Trees
Water

Concerns

Disabled access is questionable

Fee—$5

Small dogs have park without large dogs for a very limited time

Local Veterinary Clinic

Analy Veterinary Hospital
Sebastopol

707-823-7614

Ernest Holman Dog Park

151 First Street East
(next to Police Station)

Great little park! Redwood trees abound and provide complete shade.

Ernest was a little dog that is now memorialized in the park with a small statue. This is a well-used park judging by the running divots in the park surface.

This park made me sit down and look up at the gorgeous trees, and I almost went to sleep (not a good idea in a dog park). Only a few small dogs when we visited.

A quiet neighborhood—divine park.

Amenities

Bulletin board
Clean-up
Double-gated
Entrances: 4
Fenced
Grass/dirt/chips
Parking
Seating
Trees
Water

Local Veterinary Clinic

Redwood Veterinary Clinic
Santa Rosa

707-542-4012

Concerns

No small dog area

No disabled access

No restroom

Ernie Smith Dog Play Area

18776 Gillman Drive &
Bowen Court

This park is very exposed except for a few young trees on the perimeter.

One thing I didn't like was that each of the picnic tables had metal loops at the base to tie your dog next to you at the table, a problem where a dog may then be out in the direct sun, not to mention being vulnerable to other dogs.

This is a small park, and when we visited there were only a few people with their dogs, probably due to the heat.

We may try this one again when we are in the area.

Amenities

Clean-up
Double-gated
Entrances: 2
Fenced
Grass/dirt
Parking
Restroom
Seating
Trees
Water

Concerns

Rattlesnake area

No disabled access

No small dog area

Tables cemented to area not under shade trees

Local Veterinary Clinic

Redwood Veterinary Clinic
Santa Rosa

707-542-4012

Pleasant Oak Dog Park

Old Redwood Hwy. & Pleasant Ave.
(inside Pleasant Oak Park)

The fencing is cyclone, with wood slats intertwined.

A very barren plain park, but the community was great! People are involved in trying to improve the park —shade structure/trees, grass instead of the dusty chips that can be choking when dogs run and slide.

I felt very comfortable and look forward to the improvements. I will return here. Great people.

An example of a barren park that has great potential.

Amenities

Clean-up
Double-gated
Entrances: 1
Fenced
Chips
Parking
Restroom
Seating
Trees
Water

Concerns

Flooding

No shade

No disabled access

Can be very hot and dusty

No small dog area

Local Veterinary Clinic

Windsor Oaks Veterinary Clinic
Windsor

707-837-8101

Tulare County

Cody Kelly Bark Park

Plaza Drive & Airport Road
(next to Plaza Park)

The park is sweet, but there were so many young toddlers walking and falling and running and pulling at dogs, it made me nervous.

No one was using the small dog area— all dogs big and small were sharing the large dog area. The whole atmosphere felt unsafe and not policed by users.

Perhaps I hit it at an off time, but I'm hoping that this atmosphere was unique and not the norm.

The environment was very pretty, and right next to a busy duck pond.

Special Hours: 24 hours

Local Veterinary Clinic

Care Veterinary Clinic
Visalia

559-625-8549

Amenities

Bulletin board
Clean-up
Disabled access
Double-gated
Entrances: 1
Fenced
Grass/dirt
Restroom
Seating
Small dog area
Trees
Water

Concerns

For children the age limit is posted at 10 years old, but there were several toddlers trying to play with the dogs

Seven Oaks Bark Park

Tulare Ave.,
south of Ben Maddox Way

Very small park but extremely friendly community. Felt like a cozy place to spend some time.

When we were there, during off-peak hours, there were quite a few people and their dogs.

Be cautious about walking your dog to the gate entrance—it is a very busy street. Definitely, we would return to this park—Twyla apparently thought the smells were very intriguing.

Amenities

Bulletin board
Clean-up
Double-gated
Entrances: 1
Fenced
Grass/dirt
Seating
Trees
Water

Concerns

Busy street

No disabled access

No restroom

No small dog area

Local Veterinary Clinic

Care Veterinary Clinic
Visalia

559-625-8549

Ventura County

Camarillo Grove Park Dog Park

6968 E. Camarillo Springs Road

I felt like I was going into someone's private vineyard here, but I kept driving and was amply rewarded. Beautiful park inside a beautiful park. This is definitely a favorite. I'd love to give it a jumping "icon," but I found no small dog area or disabled areas inside the park.

This park atmosphere caused me to take deep breaths and relax. It is full of incredible old trees, and so inviting. I wanted to stay for hours. If I listened carefully I could hear sheep baaing in the background. It smelled like the woods.

Shady, dirt surface, long and great for ball throwing. I'll be back.

Amenities

Clean-up
Double-gated
Entrances: 2
Fenced
Dirt
Parking
Restroom
Seating
Trees
Water

Concerns

No disabled access except outside of dog area

No small dog area

Rattlesnake area

Occasional wasps

Local Veterinary Clinic

Las Posas Veterinary Medical
Camarillo

805-987-6587

Mitchell Edelson Dog Park

Soule Park Road & Bordman

This park was just a young-un when we visited—it was exactly two weeks old. Inside there are huge oak trees that provide welcome shade on a hot day.

We were greeted by a few enthusiastic small dogs, and Twyla ran and ran despite the heat that day.

The people who founded this park are extremely proud of the work they did to get this park approved, and they have been diligent about cleanliness.

I look forward to visiting again when the park is in adolescence! Good job!

Amenities

Bulletin board
Clean-up
Double-gated
Entrances: 2
Fenced
Dirt/chips
Parking
Restroom
Seating
Small dog area
Trees
Water

Concerns

Fee: $3

No disabled access

Local Veterinary Clinic

Humane Society of
Ventura County
Ojai

805-656-5031

Annie Dransfeldt Dog Park

Dean Drive & Varsity Street
(inside Camino Real Park)

This park is another favorite. It is full of big shade trees, and very friendly people. I was directed by several people to the locations of other parks in the area that I had been unaware of.

The small dog area is somewhat obsolete, not used by small dog owners much. It has become an area more for aggressive, shy, or elderly dogs that don't fit into the common fray.

We spent quite a bit of time in this park—Twyla followed around a huge gentle Great Dane named Buddy throughout the enclosure.

Amenities

Bulletin board
Clean-up
Disabled access
Double-gated
Entrances: 2
Fenced
Grass/dirt/chips
Parking
Restroom
Seating
Small dog area
Trees
Water

Concerns

Small dog area exists but is very small—no room to run

Local Veterinary Clinic

Bristol Animal Hospital
Ventura

805-656-2287

Yolo County

Community Park Dog Park

Covell Blvd. near F Street

Wow, was I disappointed!

There is no sign to tell you where you are going. It is very difficult to find— we walked all the way through the park to find a very small fenced grass area with absolutely nothing in it.

It was shady. That's it. I was hard-pressed to find any signs of use, and the label on the gate was two words: Dog Area.

We stayed about three minutes, and took off for the next park.

Amenities

Entrances: 1
Fenced
Grass/dirt
Parking
Restroom
Trees

Concerns

Hard to find—
no signs

No small dog area

No water

No clean up

No disabled access

No seating

Local Veterinary Clinic

University of California
School of Veterinary Medicine
Davis

530-752-1393

Toad Hollow Dog Park

1919 Second Street

There are lots of dog lovers in Davis—
the University of California School of
Veterinary Medicine is located here.

This is a nice large park with plenty of
stretch-out room. The trees are still
fairly young, so the best shade is from
trees that sit right outside the fence.

While most of the folks were friendly,
the size of the park can easily isolate
people or small groups of people.

We had fun, though, and Twyla
appeared to like this park—apparently
great dog smells!

Amenities

Bulletin board
Clean-up
Disabled access
Double-gated
Entrances: 1
Fenced
Grass
Parking
Seating
Water

Concerns

Flooding

No restroom

No small dog area

No specific day
for maintenance so
it's the luck of the
draw

Local Veterinary Clinic

University of California
School of Veterinary Medicine
Davis

530-752-1393

Woodland Dog Park

East Street near Road 24A

A brand new park, barely six months old when we visited. Very nice park. However, the large dog area was closed for maintenance, so all the dogs use the small dog side. It was a bit crowded for the number of dogs there on the evening we were there.

The grass is sloped (hilly) but nowhere do you lose sight of your dog.

The community here was very warm and welcoming and made Twyla and I very much a part of the group.

We will be back!

Amenities

Bulletin boards
Clean-up
Disabled access
Double-gated
Entrances: 2
Fenced
Grass/asphalt
Lights
Parking
Seating
Small dog area
Trees
Water

Concerns

No shade

Restroom inside Community Center

Local Veterinary Clinic

Valley Oak Veterinary Hospital
Woodland

530-661-6810

Amenities Glossary

Agility equipment: Jumps, tunnels, tires, A-frames, etc. like the equipment used in agility competition.

Bulletin boards: Display areas for event notices, cautions, public education and advertising.

Clean-up: Poop bags, scoopers, and /or garbage cans are provided in the park.

Disabled access: Ground cover or walkways which allow easy access for people in wheelchairs or with other mobility challenges.

Dog: The four-footer that is the reason you entered the enclosure, took off the leash, wiped the bottom of your shoe off in the grass and then went home to bathe — both of you.

Double-gated: Entrance has a first gate to let the dog in to the staging area or "take-the-leash-off area," then another gate is there to allow you to enter the dog play area.

Entrances: The number of places you can enter or exit the park.

Fenced: Fully enclosed with fencing—cyclone, wood, cement or any other material —used for confinement to the designated dog park area.

Grass/dirt/chips/gravel/asphalt: Ground cover inside the park.

Interrupters: Trees, tables, mounds, play structures and more that break up a flat open park, helpful in keeping prey drive and kinetic response in the dogs more adequately controlled.

Large dog area (sometimes called the **"common area"**):
A specific area generally designated for dogs over a certain weight, but is often used for all sizes of dogs, particularly if there is no small dog area.

Lights: Lighting provided so the park can be used safely after dark, often using street or sports lights.

Parking: A specific lot or area is provided off the street to park your car while visiting the park.

Restroom: Stand-alone building or a smelly porta-potty available, for people.

Seating: Benches or tables as well as outdoor chairs available inside the park. *(Side note: I have become a fan of minimal and uncomfortable seating or no seats at all—seating can cause people to become complacent—socializing or reading and such, minimizing the attention and time given to watching their dogs consistently and diligently.)*

Shade structure: Gazebo or other structure designed especially to keep people and dogs out of the weather.

Small dog area: A specific area for small dogs only, generally requiring a specific height or weight limit as posted on a sign at the entrance to the area.

Special Hours: Open dawn-dusk unless otherwise noted.

Trees: Large or small trees inside the enclosure or along outside perimeter providing shade. (Don't depend on all trees providing shade. In new or reconfigured parks, trees may be very young.)

Wading pools: Plastic "kiddie pools" or tubs provided for splashing, drinking and soaking (the dogs, not the people—no need for a bathing suit).

Water: Water spigots, hoses or fountains provided inside the enclosure for dogs to drink, drip, drool, splash or spread.

Cities Not Included

You may notice that a few cities are not included because of restrictions the laws put on dog run areas. Two examples:

Piedmont, California:

All parks in Piedmont, fenced or not, are accessible with your dog only when you obtain a Police Department permit. Not to mention, fenced areas are rare.

Santa Monica, California:

All dog parks in this city are for dogs licensed in Santa Monica only. As an outside visitor you will be cited, unless you spend the time and money to register your dog with the city and obtain a Santa Monica dog license. The catch-22: you have to live in the city to get the dog license. I was told by Animal Control/Santa Monica Police that I could not enter the parks with Twyla for even 15 minutes, even to research this book, without the risk of being cited.

Be aware of local ordinances
that may affect your visit with your dog.

Unfenced Areas

Unfenced dog areas are safe for some dogs, but not all. Some examples of off-leash open areas:

San Francisco:

Fort Funston has open beach and cliffs. This is a wonderful romping area for dogs and people. The paved walkway down to the beach from the parking lot is as scenic as the beach itself. This incredibly popular area is used by pooches from all over the Bay Area. Many dog meet-ups happen here for group walks on the weekends. Take a camera and dress in layers—it is, after all, San Francisco.

Mill Valley:

Mill Valley Dog Park is a beautifully landscaped park nestled in the middle of a large community park. It is unfenced, and has a San Francisco Bay inlet bordering three sides. It is quite large, grassy and well loved by park-goers. It shares the western border with a bike path, so take the longer path on the eastern field to be safe.

Multi-Use Parks

I'm not a big fan of multi-use parks—parks that post a designated day or time that dogs can play off-leash in an enclosed area that is also used as soccer or softball fields. Cleanliness is a concern: dogs leave drool, urine and feces; people leave drool, lollipop sticks and cigarette butts.

If you are going to visit a multi-use park, however, here is an example of the ideal set-up.

Menlo Park: Nealon Community Park

The softball field is used as an off-leash area Monday through Friday from 8:00 —10:00 am through an agreement with the City of Menlo Park.

Policing by the park users is tight— if you don't happen to see your dog pooping, you will hear voices calling out the description of your dog and the reason that you should be paying attention. If you cannot find the offending mass, other park users will be happy to walk over and point it out to you.

At the end of the scheduled morning period, volunteers are assigned specific days to scour the field to pick up any leftovers, and on a regular basis a "professional" is hired to go through the park after the dogs have all gone home, and scoop anything the volunteers may have missed.

Twyla and I frequent this park on a regular basis. The people are wonderful, and most of the dogs are very well-behaved.

Private Dog Parks

Private dog parks are available in at least two different venues:

> 1. Private or gated communities that are used exclusively by residents.

> 2. Parks that are owned and maintained by businesses—trainers, dog day care operators, groomers, retail establishments and more. Generally these parks require a fee for exclusive use and memberships.

Here is an example of a membership opportunity for a fee:

Petaluma:

Dairydell Canine—Maddie's Mountain. This private park is part of a training, boarding and grooming "ranch." Members pay a fee to use the park at designated times, with very specific rules. It is maintained and overseen by the proprietors and membership may be approved, revoked or refused at their discretion.

The advantage: dogs are carefully screened before membership is granted, guaranteeing increased safety and extensive knowledge of each of the dogs (and the people) that are using the park.

Disadvantage: some dogs and people are excluded that actually need the space and socializing opportunities afforded by community parks, and there may be limited or no other parks in the area.

Resources

BOOKS:

Donaldson, Jean: *The Culture Clash* (James & Kenneth Publishers)

Donaldson, Jean: *Oh Behave!* (Dogwise Publishing)

Goodavage, Maria: *The Dog Lover's Companion to California* (Avalon Travel Publishing)

Goodavage, Maria: *The Dog Lover's Companion to the Bay Area* (Avalon Travel Publishing)

King, Trish: *Dogsense* (Marin Humane Society)

King, Trish: *Parenting Your Dog* (T.F.H. Publications, Inc.)

Smith, Cheryl: *Visiting the Dog Park: Having Fun, Staying Safe* (Dogwise Publishing)

WEBSITES: www.berrygrovedogs.com

Bark.com
Baywoof.com
Bravopup.com
CanineCreek.com
Dogfriendly.com
Dogparks.org
Dogparkusa.com
Dogplay.com
Dogster.com
Dogwise.com
Fetchthepaper.com

Fundawgs.com
JeanDonaldson.com
MarinHumaneSociety.org
Petlane.com
SFSPCA.org
Usadogparks.com
Woofreport.com

Disabled Access and Small Dog Areas

d = Disabled Access
s = Small Dog Area

Alameda
    Alameda Dog Park d,s
    Alameda Point Dog Run d
Aptos
    Polo Grounds Dog Park   d,s
Arcadia
    Eisenhower Memorial Dog Park d,s
Arroyo Grande
    Elm Street Off-leash Dog Park d,s
Auburn
    Ashley Memorial Park d,s
Bakersfield
    Silver Creek Small Dog Park s
Belmont
    Ciprianni Dog Park d,s
Benicia
    Phoenix Community Dog Park d,s
Berkeley
    Ohlone Dog Park d
Brentwood (Los Angeles)
    Barrington Dog Park d,s
Brisbane
    Brisbane Dog Park d
Burlingame
    Bayside Park Dog Exercise Area s
Calabasas
    Calabasas Bark Park s
Campbell
    Los Gatos Creek Park Dog Park d,s
Carmichael
    Carmichael Park Canine Corral d,s
Castro Valley
    Earl Warren Dog Park s

Chico
        DeGarmo Dog Park d
Chula Vista
        Montevalle Dog Park d,s
Citrus Heights
        C-Bar-C Park s
Claremont
        Claremont Pooch Park d,s
Clayton
        Clayton Dog Park d
Concord
        The Paw Patch d,s
Corona
        Butterfield Dog Park s,d
        Harada Heritage Dog Park (Eastvale) d,s
Costa Mesa
        Costa Mesa Bark Park d
Culver City
        The Boneyard d,s
Danville
        Canine Corral Dog Park d,s
Davis
        Toad Hollow Dog Park d
Dublin
        Dougherty Hills Dog Park d,s
El Cajon
        Well's Park Dog Park d,s
El Cerrito
        Pt. Isabel Regional Park Dog Run d
El Segundo
        El Segundo Dog Park s
Elk Grove
        Laguna Dog Park d
Encinitas
        Rancho Coastal Humane Society Dog Park d,s
Encino
        Sepulveda Basin Dog Park d
Escondido
        Mayflower Dog Park d,s
Fair Oaks
        Phoenix Dog Park s
Folsom
        FIDO Field d,s

Foster City
        Foster City Dog Run d,s
Fremont
        Central Park Dog Park d
        Lake Elizabeth Dog Park d
Fresno
        El Capitan Dog Park d
        Woodward Dog Park d
Fullerton
        Pooch Park d,s
Galt
        Kiwanis Dog Park d,s
Hanford
        Freedom Park d,s
Healdsburg
        Badger Dog Park s
Highland
        Highland Dog Park d
Hollywood/Studio City
        Laurel Canyon Dog Park s
Huntington Beach
        Best Friend Dog Park d,s
Irvine
        Central Bark Dog Park d,s
La Mesa
        Harry Griffen Dog Park s
Laguna Beach
        Laguna Beach Bark Park d,s
Laguna Nigel
        Laguna Niguel Dog Park s
Laguna Woods
        Laguna Woods Dog Park s
Lancaster
        Forrest E. Hull Dog Park d,s
Larkspur
        Canine Commons s
Livermore
        Max Baer Dog Park d
        Marlin A. Pound Dog Park (Springtown Dog Park) d,s
Loma Linda
        Loma Linda Dog Park s
Long Beach
        Long Beach Recreation Dog Park d,s

Los Angeles
    Griffith Park Dog Park d
    Hermon Dog Park d,s
    Silver Lake Dog Park s
Menlo Park
    Nealon Community Park d
    Willow Oak Park Dog Park d
Milpitas
    Milpitas Dog Park d,s
Morgan Hill
    Morgan Hill Off-leash Dog Park d,s
Mountain View
    Mountain View Dog Park d,s
Napa
    Canine Commons s
Natomas
    Tanzanite Dog Park d,s
North Hollywood
    Whitnall Dog Park d,s
North Natomas
    Regency Dog Park d
Novato
    Dog Bone Meadow d
    Marin Humane Society Dog Park d,s
Oakland
    Hardy Dog Park d
    Joaquin Miller Dog Park s
    Mosswood Dog Park d,s
Oceanside
    North Coastal Humane Society Off-leash Dog Park d,s
Ojai
    Mitchell Edelson Dog Park s
Orange
    Orange Dog Park d,s
Palm Desert
    Civic Center Dog Park d,s
    Freedom Dog Park d,s
    Joe Mann Dog Park d,s
Palm Springs
    Palm Springs Dog Park d,s
Palo Alto
    Greer Park – Pup'n'Run d
Pasadena
    Alice's Dog Park d,s

Petaluma
      Rocky Memorial Park d
Pinole
      Pinole Valley Dog Park s
Pleasant Hill
      Paso Nogal Dog Park d,s
Pleasanton
      Muirwood Dog Park s
Poway
      Poway Dog Park d,s
Rancho Cucamonga
      Rancho Cucamonga Dog Park d,s
Redding
      Benton Park- Redding Dog Park d,s
Redondo Beach
      Redondo Beach Dog Park d,s
Redwood City
      Shores Dog Park s
Riverside
      Pat Merritt Dog Park s
      Riverwalk Dog Park s
Rohnert Park
      Rohnert Park Dog Park s
Roseville
      Bear Dog Park d,s
      Marco Dog Park d
      William Hughes Park Dog Park s
Sacramento
      Bannon Creek Dog Park d
      Granite Dog Park d
      Howe About Dogs d
      Partner Park d
San Bernadino
      Wildwood Dog Park s
San Bruno
      Commodore Dog Run d,s
San Clemente
      Baron von Willard Memorial Dog Park s
San Diego
      Capeheart Dog Park d,s
      Doyle Community Park Dog Park s
      Maddox Park Dog Park d
      Nobel Dog Park d,s

San Diego
  Rancho Bernardo Off-leash Park d,s
  Torrey Highlands Dog Park d
San Dimas
  San Dimas Dog Park d,s
San Francisco
  Eureka Valley Dog Park d
  Golden Gate Park Dog Run d
  St. Mary's Dog Park d
  Upper Noe Dog Park d
  Walter Haas Playground Dog Park d
San Jose
  Butcher Dog Park d,s
  Delmas Dog Park d
  Fontana Dog Park d,s
  Hellyer Park Dog Run d
  Miyuki Dog Park d,s
  Ryland Dog Park d
  Saratoga Creek Dog Park d
  Watson Dog Park s
San Lorenzo
  San Lorenzo Dog Park d,s
San Luis Obispo
  Elm Street Off-leash Dog Park d,s
  El Chorro Park Dog Park d,s
San Mateo
  Seal Point Dog Run d
San Pedro
  Knoll Hill Dog Park d,s
San Rafael
  Field of Dogs d,s
San Ramon
  Bollinger Dog Run d,s
Santa Clara
  Reed Street Dog Park d,s
Santa Maria
  WOOF Pac Park d,s
Santa Rosa
  Doyle Dog Park d,s
  DeTurk Round Barn Park d
  Galvin Dog Park d
  Northwest Community Dog Park s
  Rincon Community Park d,s

Scotts Valley
    Scotts Valley Dog Park d,s
Sebastopol
    Ragle Ranch Animal Care Center Park s
Sierra Madre
    Sierra Madre Dog Park s
Stockton
    Barkleyville Dog Park d,s
Studio City/Hollywood
    Laurel Canyon Dog Park s
Tehachapi
    Meadowbrook Dog Park s
Temecula
    Temecula Dog Exercise Area s
Thousand Oaks
    Conejo Creek Dog Park d,s
Tracy
    Cora K-9 Facility Dog Park d,s
Union City
    Drigon Dog Park d,s
Upland
    Baldy View Dog Park s
Vacaville
    Vacaville Dog Park d
Vallejo
    Wardlaw Park Dog Park d,s
Venice
    Westminster Dog Park s
Ventura
    Annie Dransfeldt Dog Park d,s
Visalia
    Cody Kelly Bark Park d,s
Walnut Creek
    Wag World Dog Park, Heather Farm Park d,s
Watsonville
    Watsonville Dog Park d,s
West Hollywood
    William S. Hart Dog Park d
West Sacramento
    Sam Combs Dog Park d,s
Woodland
    Woodland Dog Park d,s

About the Author

Gail S. Green, CPDT, has worked with some of the most innovative trainers across the country. Many dogs, cats, birds and pocket pets have shared Gail's life and each has provided hands-on experience that has contributed to the formation of her strong convictions and beliefs about how animals must be treated. Gail is passionate about and active in rescue work. She has coached hundreds of volunteers of all ages in animal shelters and community programs to assist in the prevention of pet homelessness. She is active in service animal advocacy, as well as founder of a prominent volunteer animal -assisted therapy group, TherapyPets, Inc. She is also the co-founder of the first designated fenced dog park in the U.S., Ohlone Dog Park in Berkeley.

A life-changing event in Gail's life was her involvement in the animal rescue efforts when she headed to Louisiana and Mississippi following the devastating Hurricane Katrina. She has become a strong promoter of animal and pet disaster preparation and response. She has authored numerous articles and lectured on companion animal behavior, animal-assisted therapy and her experiences in the Gulf Coast.

She grew up in Berkeley in a close-knit family of eight. Gail now lives in Richmond, California with Dannie, her partner and spouse of 23 years; her amazing and funny parakeet, Hatch; and her opinionated and silly side-kick—a Border Terrier mix, Twyla.

CPSIA information can be obtained at www.ICGtesting.com
Printed in the USA
LVOW130601140612

285920LV00006B/54/P